Good Night *in* Guide

D1077920

Barry Norman

Journalist, broadcaster and novelist. Best known as BBC TV's film critic for the past 20 years. Barry lives in a small village in Hertfordshire with his wife Diana.

Emma Norman

Barry's youngest of two daughters. Emma is a freelance journalist and regularly reviews videos on GLR (BBC London) and Radio 5 as well as making increasingly more appearances on TV. She lives in North West London.

There are so many films available on video now that it's practically impossible to sort your way through them without a movie guide. Well, fine there are plenty of comprehensive guides available but they tend to be on the large side and when you pop into the video store after that Saturday morning raid on the supermarket you don't necessarily want to be carrying a thumping great book about. Hence "The Good Night *in* Guide" which is designed most of all to be user-friendly. We've included a brief synopsis of what the movies are about and/or who's in them and who directed them .... we've rated them from * (OK) to ***** (not to be missed) .... and we've put them into ten categories ranging from comedy to horror to action/adventure. That was the tough bit. If you think about it, the number of categories into which movies can fall are almost endless. Take 'Casablanca' as just one example. Depending on your point of view it could be action/adventure or drama, so we put it in both. Hence the categories are simply a broad rule of thumb to give you a rough idea of the kind of film you're about to take home or maybe reject.

At the front of the book you will find not ten but eleven lists of recommended films under different category headings. (As a bonus, no extra charge, we threw in ten first-rate war movies). These lists should not in any way be interpreted as our choice of the all-time greatest in any category. They merely reflect (after much discussion and argument) our joint selection of particularly watchable films from those that are, or should be, readily available on video.

What we have tried to do throughout the guide is to name only the movies that a good video store will stock or will be able to get for you. Pointless to list films that should be readily available on video but aren't. This means we have excluded several greats such as The Producers, Midnight Cowboy, The Gunfighter and Duck Soup. However, we are confident that those we have recommended will provide you with a great deal of pleasure. And at the very least our selections should stimulate argument and maybe inspire you to while away a few hours by drawing up your own top ten. This is an exercise guaranteed to enliven any quiet evening and set children against parents, husband against wife, friend against friend. In any event we hope "The Good Night *in* Guide" will help you find a way through that dense forest of videos. Keep it with you and we don't think you'll go far wrong.

Happy viewing.

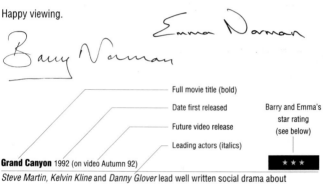

Full movie title (bold)

Date first released

Future video release

Leading actors (italics)

Barry and Emma's star rating (see below)

★ ★ ★

Grand Canyon 1992 (on video Autumn 92)

Steve Martin, Kelvin Kline and *Danny Glover* lead well written social drama about problems of living in modern, violent LA.

Not to be missed	★ ★ ★ ★ ★
Excellent	★ ★ ★ ★
Very good	★ ★ ★
Worth watching	★ ★
OK	★

TOP TENS

These are our recommendations for ten special videos in each genre which should be readily available, or at least easily obtainable by your local store. There are of course many other great films we would have liked to include, but for one reason or another they are sadly less easy to find on video.

The more astute of you will notice that we have slipped in an extra genre. War films are in fact included largely within the Action/Adventure section of the guide itself.

ACTION / ADVENTURE

The Adventures of Robin Hood (1938)
Lawrence of Arabia
The Godfather
Jaws
Thelma & Louise
The African Queen
Romancing the Stone
Indiana Jones Trilogy
48 Hours
The Untouchables

COMEDY

Bringing Up Baby
To Be or Not to Be (1942)
Life is Sweet
Gregory's Girl
The Man with Two Brains
Tootsie
Ninotchka
A Fish Called Wanda
The Life of Brian
Whisky Galore

DRAMA

Citizen Kane
Gone with the Wind
Casablanca
The Third Man
Raging Bull
All About Eve
The Red Shoes
One Flew over the Cuckoo's Nest
Midnight Express
Henry V (1989)

FAMILY

The Wizard Of Oz
It's a Wonderful Life
The Railway Children
Great Expectations (1946)
Crocodile Dundee
Local Hero
Moonstruck
Field of Dreams
The Prisoner of Zenda
Home Alone

FOREIGN

La Regle du Jeu
Ran
The Seven Samurai
Cyrano de Bergerac (1991)
Pelle the Conqueror
The Nasty Girl
The Seventh Seal
Jean de Florette / Manon des Sources
Cinema Paradiso
Toto the Hero

HORROR

The Silence of the Lambs

Psycho

An American Werewolf in London

Misery

The Omen

Cape Fear (1991)

The Hitcher

Halloween

A Nightmare on Elm Street

Carrie

MUSICALS

Singin' in the Rain

High Society

Kiss Me Kate

Cabaret

The King and I

The Commitments

Seven Brides for Seven Brothers

Showboat

The Sound of Music

Oliver!

MYSTERY / THRILLER

The Maltese Falcon

Witness

Jagged Edge

The Thirty Nine Steps (1935)

Chinatown

Klute

Someone to Watch Over Me

Laura

Suspect

In the Heat of the Night

SCI FI / FANTASY

E.T., the Extra-Terrestrial

Close Encounters of the Third Kind

2001: A Space Odyssey

Star Wars Trilogy

Terminator II

Back to the Future Trilogy

Alien / Aliens

Total Recall

Superman 2

Ghostbusters

WAR

Apocalypse Now

The Cruel Sea

M*A*S*H

The Bridge on the River Kwai

The Great Escape

Platoon

The Dam Busters

A Bridge Too Far

Zulu

All Quiet on the Western Front

WESTERNS

The Searchers

Stage Coach

Butch Cassidy and the Sundance Kid

High Noon

Shane

The Magnificent Seven

Dances with Wolves

Red River

The Outlaw Josey Wales

The Wild Bunch

Above Us the Waves 1956

Gripping wartime drama of British submarine crew attempting to destroy enemy ship. *John Mills* tops impressive cast list.

Adventures of Robin Hood, The 1938

Glorious swashbuckler with *Errol Flynn* as the dashing outlaw, *Olivia de Haviland*, a feisty Maid Marion and *Claud Rains*, the evil Prince John.

Adventures of Robin Hood, The 1991

Lacklustre version of Norman vs Saxon folklore. *Patrick Bergin's* Robin lacks magnetism.

African Queen, The 1951

Magnificent romantic adventure as prissy missionary, *Katherine Hepburn*, and drunken captain, *Humphrey Bogart*, brave treacherous river journey to destroy Nazi battleship.

Air America 1990

Mel Gibson and *Robert Downey Jnr.* as C.I.A. pilots in Vietnam. Weak on the comedy; goodish action.

All Quiet on the Western Front 1930

Outstanding WWI drama examining the disillusionment of young soldiers in the trenches.

Another 48 Hours 1990

Eddie Murphy and *Nick Nolte's* continuing love/hate relationship as they take on The Iceman. Not a patch on the original.

Apocalypse Now 1979

Francis Coppola's hypnotic version of Joseph Conrad's 'Heart of Darkness', set in Vietnam. Poignantly played by *Martin Sheen, Robert Duvall* and *Marlon Brando*.

Assault on Precinct 13 1976

John Carpenter's impressive modern-day 'Rio Bravo' set in L.A. police station besieged by gang of youths.

Backdraft 1991

Feuding firemen brothers, *Kurt Russell* and *William Baldwin*, fight arsonist and each other. Mediocre story, spectacular fire sequences.

Batman 1989

Michael Keaton's moody hero overshadowed by _Jack Nicholson's_ hammy Joker. Dark and impressive sets.

Ben Hur 1959

William Wyler's eleven Oscar epic pits _Charlton Heston's_ revenge seeking galley slave against Romans. Marvellous chariot race.

Beverley Hills Cop 1984

Fast-talking, wise-cracking cop, _Eddie Murphy,_ takes L.A. vacation to find friend's killer. Great undemanding stuff.

Big Easy, The 1987

Offbeat, New Orleans cop, _Dennis Quaid,_ and uptight but sexy D.A., _Ellen Barkin,_ investigate case of police corruption.

Big Heat, The 1953

Fritz Lang's notable piece of film noir about policeman, _Glenn Ford_, going under cover to get revenge on crime ring.

Billy Bathgate 1991 (on video Summer 92)

Young lad yearns to join ranks of _Dustin Hoffman's_ mob in 1930's overlong gangster story. _Bruce Willis_ and Nicole Kidman co-star.

Black Rain 1989

Ridley Scott's violent cops and robbers thriller set in Japan is tough, long and predictable. _Michael Douglas_ and _Andy Garcia._

Bonnie and Clyde 1967

Warren Beatty and _Faye Dunaway_ as violent robbers on lawless spree in classic 60's movie.

Breaker Morant 1979 ★ ★

Three Australian soldiers court-martialled for Boer war atrocities. With _Edward Woodward_ and _Jack Thompson._

Bridge on the River Kwai, The 1957 ★ ★ ★ ★ ★

David Lean's powerful drama of P.O.W.s constructing bridge for Japanese captors. _Alec Guinness_ superb.

Bridge Too Far, A 1977 ★ ★ ★ ★

Richard Attenborough's honest, star-studded portrayal of WWII Allied operation to control the Rhine.

Bullitt 1968 ★ ★ ★

Steve McQueen at his best in police drama memorable for San Francisco car chase.

Captain Blood 1935 ★ ★ ★

Doctor _Errol Flynn_ forced to become pirate. Plenty of duels, romance and sea battles.

Carve Her Name With Pride 1958 ★ ★ ★

Moving WWII biopic of young British widow, _Virginia McKenna_, enlisted as spy to help French resistance.

Casablanca 1942 ★ ★ ★ ★ ★

Classic WWII romance set in Morocco with _Humphrey Bogart_ and _Ingrid Bergman_.

Catch 22 1970 ★ ★ ★

Alan Arkin leads good cast in Mike Nichols' honourable attempt to bring Joseph Heller's brilliant anti-war novel to life.

Convoy 1978 ★ ★

Daft but amiable Sam Peckinpah story of truckers striking against oppression in trek across southwest.

Corsican Brothers, The 1941 ★ ★ ★

Twins separated at birth remain emotionally attached, in entertaining version of Alexandre Dumas adventure.

Cotton Club, The 1984 ★ ★

Francis Coppolla's flawed but vivid drama centred on famous Harlem nightclub and rise of the Mafia.

Cruel Sea, The 1953 ★ ★ ★ ★

Gripping action adventure involving the crew of a warship during WWII. Among the best of British war films.

Dam Busters, The 1954

Host of English actors grace exciting, intelligent WWII tale of Barnes Wallace and his bouncing bomb.

Days of Thunder 1990

Tom Cruise and *Nicole Kidman* in a 'Top Gun' set among car racers. Very flashy; little substance.

D-Day, the Sixth of June 1956

Lengthy account of WWII Normandy invasion. *Robert Taylor* leads the troops.

Dead-Bang 1989

Don Johnson's best performance as detective uncovering run-of-the-mill conspiracy.

Dead Pool, The 1988

Dirty Harry (*Clint Eastwood*) in fifth outing; here investigating bizarre death list.

Deliverance 1972

Horrifying events overtake *Burt Reynolds* and friends on canoe trip through hill-billy country. Probably Reynolds' best performance.

Desert Fox, The 1951

James Mason portrays Field Marshal Rommel facing defeat, disillusionment and death.

Desert Rats, The 1953

Good star-studded tale of British captain, *Richard Burton*, warding off German troops in North Africa. *Mason* plays Rommel again.

Desperate Hours, The 1990

Michael Cimino's violent but dullish remake features *Mickey Rourke* as escaped psycho holing up with *Anthony Hopkins* and family.

Diamonds are Forever 1971

Sean Connery's penultimate outing as 007, this time in Las Vegas. With *Jill St. John* and *Charles Gray.*

Dick Tracy 1990   ★ ★ ★

Warren Beatty's visually splendid version of gang-busting comic book hero. *Al Pacino* steals show.

Die Hard 1988   ★ ★ ★ ★

Excellent action drama stars *Bruce Willis* as wise-cracking cop single-handedly battling terrorists. *Alan Rickman* makes great heavy.

Die Hard 2 1990   ★ ★

Willis returns to take on terrorists who've hijacked airport. Same as before but not as good.

Dirty Dozen, The 1967   ★ ★ ★

Macho, starry cast play hard-case jailbirds sent to infiltrate enemy lines to redeem themselves.

Dirty Harry 1971   ★ ★ ★

First and best outing for *Clint Eastwood* as sharp-shooting detective assigned to bring in crazed killer.

Driver, The 1978   ★ ★

Car chases best thing in action drama with *Ryan O'Neal* as professional getaway driver up against cop, *Bruce Dern*.

Dr No 1962   ★ ★

First of the Bond movies sees *Sean Connery* creating 007. Still one of the best.

Eagle has Landed, The 1977   ★ ★

Nazi plot to assassinate Churchill provides reasonable star vehicle for likes of *Michael Caine, Robert Duvall* and *Donald Sutherland*.

El Cid 1961   ★ ★ ★

Spectacular action movie sees the Spanish hero, *Charlton Heston*, romancing *Sophia Loren* as he drives the Moors from his country.

Electra Glide in Blue 1973   ★ ★

Well-plotted violent thriller. *Robert Black* rises from diminutive status as traffic cop to plain-clothes detective on a murder hunt.

Emerald Forest, The 1985

Based on true adventure of man's ten-year struggle to recover kidnapped son from Amazon Jungle. John Boorman directed.

Enforcer, The 1976

Dirty Harry Callahan (*Clint Eastwood*) and female partner, *Tyne Daly*, on trail of terrorists.

Escape from Alcatraz 1979

Reasonable action yarn with *Clint Eastwood* escaping from the reputedly ultra-secure prison in story based on fact.

Escape from Sobibor 1987

Alan Arkin leads biggest escape ever attempted from a Nazi concentration camp in solid, made-for-TV movie.

Exterminator, The 1980

Violent vigilante, *Robert Ginty*, wreaking revenge on gang that paralysed friend.

First of the Few, The 1942

Impressive biopic depicting life of R. J. Mitchell and events surrounding his invention of the Spitfire.

48 Hours 1982

Sharp, fast thriller in which cop, *Nick Nolte*, borrows jailed con-man, *Eddie Murphy*, for a two day attempt to catch vicious cop killer.

For Your Eyes Only 1981

Roger Moore as 007. Stunts and traditional action replace earlier technical wizardry.

French Connection, The 1971

Narcotics cops, *Gene Hackman* and *Roy Scheider*, fighting heroin importers in N.Y.. Good action movie with exceptional car chase.

French Connection II 1975

Hackman reprises role of Popeye Doyle - this time in Paris - in acceptable sequel.

From Russia with Love 1963　　　　　　　

Sean Connery as James Bond nicely supported by *Robert Shaw* as psycho assassin.

Gallipoli 1981　　　　　　★ ★ ★ ★

Gripping study of the people and events involved in futile, suicidal WWI Australian campaign against Turks. *Mel Gibson* at best under Peter Weir's direction.

Gambler, The 1974　　　　　　★ ★ ★

Tense drama about a compulsive gambler expertly played by *James Caan*.

Gauntlet, The 1977　　　　　　★ ★ ★

Fast-paced action movie directed by and starring *Clint Eastwood*, as cop escorting prostitute, *Sondra Locke*, to testify at trial.

Gleaming the Cube 1989　　　　　　★

Silly murder/mystery for teenage *Christian Slater* to investigate. Skateboard stunts make it worth watching.

Gloria 1980　　　　　　

Gena Rowlands in title role of tough, savvy housewife protecting orphan boy from Mafia.

Glory 1989　　　　　　★ ★ ★ ★

Harrowing account of first black regiment in American civil war. *Matthew Broderick* and *Denzel Washington* excellent as are battle scenes.

Godfather, The 1972　　　　　　★ ★ ★ ★ ★

Best gangster movie ever made. Definitive Mafia story awash with talent. Francis Coppola directs. *Marlon Brando, Al Pacino* and *James Caan* head Corleone family.

Godfather, Part II, The 1974　　　　　　★ ★ ★ ★ ★

Only sequel to match its forerunner continues Corleone saga minus James Caan. Compelling story of corruption of power.

Godfather, Part III, The 1990　　　　　　

Most lavish but weakest of the family series. Still worth watching if only for *Andy Garcia*.

Goldfinger 1964   ★ ★ ★

Sean Connery, licensed to kill, takes on adversary, *Gert Frobe*. *Honor Blackman* the unusually feisty Bond girl.

Goodfellas 1990   ★ ★ ★ ★

Martin Scorcese's violent, riveting depiction of Mafia soldiers in New York. Explosive performance from *Joe Pesci*. *Robert De Niro* and *Ray Liotta* giving excellent support.

Great Escape, The 1963   ★ ★ ★ ★ ★

Plethora of stars play Allied P.O.W.'s masterminding mass breakout of WWII German concentration camp.

Greystoke: The Legend of Tarzan, Lord of the Apes 1984   ★ ★ ★

Rich and faithful version of the Tarzan story. *Christopher Lambert's* the man raised by apes, *Ralph Richardson* his baronial uncle bringing him home.

Gunga Din 1939   ★ ★ ★

Ripping yarn with *Cary Grant, Douglas Fairbanks Jnr.* and *Victor Maclaglan* as three soldier comrades involved in C19th uprising in India. Owes little to Rudyard Kipling.

Guns of Navarone, The 1961   ★ ★ ★

Multi-national commandos dispatched to destroy WWII German gun. Cracking action adventure with *Gregory Peck, David Niven* and *Richard Harris*.

Hard Way, The 1989   ★ ★ ★

Movie star *Michael J. Fox* attaches himself to unwelcoming, hard-nosed N.Y. cop, *James Woods*, to research a forthcoming role.

Heroes of Telemark, The 1965   ★ ★

Kirk Douglas and *Richard Harris* fight nasty Nazis over-running Norway.

Hunt for Red October, The 1990   ★ ★ ★

Exciting suspense thriller about a Soviet Captain, *Sean Connery*, using a state-of-the-art submarine to defect.

Ice Cold in Alex 1960   ★ ★ ★ ★

John Mills stranded in desert in charge of ambulance, a nurse and a Nazi soldier. Splendid WWII action adventure.

Indiana Jones and the Last Crusade 1989   ★ ★ ★ ★

Best of the series sees *Harrison Ford* searching for his father, *Sean Connery*, and the Holy Grail.

Indiana Jones and the Temple of Doom 1984   ★ ★ ★

Weakish sequel to 'Raiders of The Lost Ark'. *Harrison Ford* as Jones, *Kate Capshaw* as Jones's girl.

Innocent Man, An 1989   ★ ★

Brutal, overlong action movie. *Tom Selleck* wrongly imprisoned and out for justice and revenge.

Internal Affairs 1990   ★ ★

Crooked cop, *Richard Gere*, investigated by fellow officer, *Andy Garcia*, in tough, action drama.

In Which We Serve 1942   ★ ★ ★

Noel Coward's WWII drama about survivors of torpedoed destroyer. Dated but still splendid. *Richard Attenborough* makes his debut.

Italian Job, The 1969   ★ ★ ★

Michael Caine and *Noel Coward* in crime caper. Complicated plot involves creating world's biggest traffic jam.

Ivanhoe 1953   ★ ★

Robert Taylor as Walter Scott's chivalrous knight. *Elizabeth Taylor, Joan Fontaine* and *George Sanders* in support. Fine cinematography.

Jaws 1975   ★ ★ ★ ★ ★

Spielberg's terrific thriller of seaside resort terrorised by shark. *Roy Scheider, Robert Shaw* and *Richard Dreyfuss* as both hunters and hunted.

Jewel Of the Nile, The 1985   ★ ★

Fast-paced but slight sequel to 'Romancing The Stone'. *Kathleen Turner, Michael Douglas* and *Danny DeVito* reprise roles.

Karate Kid, The 1984   ★ ★

Bullied teenager, *Ralph Macchio*, turns on tormentors when Japanese handyman, *Pat Morita*, teaches him karate.

Key Largo 1948

Gangster *Edward G. Robinson* holds *Humphrey Bogart, Lauren Bacall* and others captive in John Huston film noir.

Kidnapped 1971

Stevenson's cracking adventure done justice by solid British cast, headed by *Michael Caine*.

Killing Fields, The 1984

Roland Joffe's sensitive account of a reporter's harrowing experience during Cambodian war packs a hefty punch.

King Kong 1976

Good special effects and sympathetic attitude towards gorilla in competent remake. *Jessica Lange's* first film.

K9 1989

Alsatian and cop, *James Belushi*, pal up to catch drug pushers in feeble action movie.

Ladyhawke 1985

Lavish fantasy based on 700-year-old legend of lovers, *Michelle Pfeiffer* and *Rutger Hauer*, separated by curse.

Last Boy Scout, The 1991 (on video Summer 92)

Ultra-violent action thriller pickled with comic one-liners and hectic car chases. *Bruce Willis* stars as down-at-heel P.I..

Lawrence of Arabia 1962

David Lean's great epic brought instant stardom for *Peter O'Toole* as the enigmatic adventurer.

Lethal Weapon 1987

Fast-action cops and robbers pairing *Mel Gibson* and *Danny Glover* as the good guys. Violent, trashy and fun.

Lethal Weapon 2 1989

Inevitable sequel to the above. Perhaps even more violent. Again *Gibson* and *Glover* risk all to catch baddies.

Light Sleeper 1991 (on video Autumn 92)   ★ ★

Susan Sarandon and *Willem Dafoe* lead this thriller set in the seedy world of drug-running.

Little Caesar 1930   ★ ★ ★

Edward G. Robinson shot to stardom in this dated but classic 1930's gangster movie.

Live and Let Die 1973   ★ ★

First licence to kill for *Roger Moore* as James Bond. Lots of wild chase sequences. Paul McCartney title song.

Lock-up 1989   ★

Violent, soppy thriller with convict, *Sylvester Stallone*, persecuted by jail governor, *Donald Sutherland*.

Longest Day, The 1962   ★ ★ ★ ★

Mammoth recreation of Allied invasion of Normandy. Stirring battle scenes and all-star cast; *John Wayne, Henry Fonda, Sean Connery, Richard Burton* etc..

Long Good Friday, The 1980   ★ ★ ★ ★

Tough, exciting British gangster thriller. Great performance by *Bob Hoskins*; fine support from *Helen Mirren*.

Mad Max 1979   ★ ★ ★

Futuristic innovative action movie. *Mel Gibson* the policeman out to avenge the murder of wife and child.

Mad Max 2 1981   ★ ★ ★

Visually impressive, action-filled sequel sees *Gibson* protecting small community against marauding gang.

Mad Max: Beyond the Thunderdome 1985   ★ ★ ★

Mel Gibson's futuristic warrior exiled to desert. Stunts, chases and *Tina Turner* flesh it out a bit.

Man Who Would be King, The 1975   ★ ★ ★ ★

Splendid John Huston version of Kipling story. *Sean Connery* and *Michael Caine* as British soldiers conning Indian priests of riches.

Marathon Man 1976

Absorbing thriller in which student, *Dustin Hoffman*, is unwittingly embroiled in hunt for Nazi war criminal, *Laurence Olivier*.

Memphis Belle 1990

Spectacular dramatization of the 25th and final mission of B52 bomber crew during WWII. Young male talent form crew.

Miami Blues 1990

Psycho criminal, *Alec Baldwin*, and naive prostitute, *Jennifer Jason Leigh*, doggedly pursued by victimized cop, *Fred Ward*. Performances better than plot.

Midnight Run 1988

Comedy/action adventure matches bounty hunter, *Robert De Niro*, against fugitive, *Charles Grodin*, whose performance steals film.

Mobsters, The Evil Empire 1991 (on video Autumn 92)

Christian Slater leads dim, Brat Pack gangster movie about the rise of Lucky Luciano.

Moonraker 1979

Roger Moore as 007 in James Bond adventure that increasingly resembles an animated comic strip.

Mutiny on the Bounty 1935

Charles Laughton superbly evil as Bligh, *Clark Gable* charismatic as the mutiny leader, Fletcher Christian.

Name of the Rose, The 1986

Atmospheric, mystery story of a Monk turned detective, *Sean Connery*, investigating murders in C14th monastery.

Narrow Margin 1990 ★ ★

Fairly tense thriller with D.A., *Gene Hackman*, trying to protect murder witness *Anne Archer* on perilous train trip through Rockies.

Never Say Never Again 1983 ★ ★ ★

Sean Connery returns as Bond in stylish but overlong remake of 'Thunderball'.

No Mercy 1986

Richard Gere, a policeman bent on revenge, distracted by pouting _Kim Basinger_ in bemusing, mediocre thriller.

Octopussy 1983

Thirteenth James Bond movie sees _Roger Moore_ smoothly outwitting the evil _Maud Adams_ and dastardly plot to nuke U.S. forces.

Once Upon a Time in America 1984

Sergio Leone's sprawling, flawed, riveting saga of Jewish gangsters in the 1920's. _Robert De Niro_ and _James Woods_ star.

Papillon 1973

Outstanding performances by _Dustin Hoffman_ and _Steve McQueen_ in overlong story of prisoner's escape from Devil's Island.

Platoon 1986

Oliver Stone's harrowing depiction of U.S. soldiers lives - and their atrocities - during Vietnam war.

Point Break 1991

Ludicrous action picture about surfing bank robbers. With _Patrick Swayze_ and _Keanu Reeves_.

Poseidon Adventure, The 1972

Disaster movie on the high seas as starry cast panic aboard sinking liner. Oscar-winning special effects.

Predator 1987

Arnold Schwarzenegger heads S.W.A.T team on rescue mission in jungle, but someone - or something - keeps killing them.

Presidio, The 1988

Formula thriller with soldier, _Sean Connery_, and cop, _Mark Harmon_, clashing during army base murder investigation.

Princess Bride, The 1987 ★ ★ ★ ★

Enchanting fairytale adventure in which abducted princess, _Robin Wright_, must be rescued by dashing hero, _Cary Elwes_.

Prisoner of Zenda, The 1952

Very acceptable re-make of classic 1937 Ronald Colman movie, this time starring *Stewart Granger*.

Public Enemy, The 1931

Splendid early gangster movie - the one in which *James Cagney* shoves a grapefruit into *Mae Clark's* face.

Quiller Memorandum, The 1966

American secret agent, *George Segal*, infiltrates neo-Nazi movement in Berlin. Enjoyable thriller.

Rage in Harlem, A 1991

Racy, sometimes effective, combination of sex and violence in quest for stolen gold in 1950's Harlem.

Raiders of the Lost Ark 1981

First rousing adventure of intrepid archaeologist Indiana Jones (*Harrison Ford*). Expertly directed by Steven Spielberg.

Raid on Entebbe 1977

Tense, well-told story of Israeli commandoes rescuing hostages held at Uganda airport. *Peter Finch* and *Charles Bronson* lead.

Reach for the Sky 1956   ★ ★ ★

Solid account of exploits of WWII flying ace Douglas Bader (*Kenneth Moore*) despite double leg amputation.

Return of the Swamp Thing 1989   ★ ★

Vegetable superhero rescues distressed damsel, *Heather Locklear*, from evil *Louis Jourdan*. Cheap and cheerful.

Roaring Twenties, The 1939   ★ ★ ★ ★

Dated but still classic gangster story. *James Cagney* and *Humphrey Bogart* involved with the rackets after WWI.

Robin and Marian 1976   ★ ★ ★ ★

Sean Connery and *Audrey Hepburn* as the now aging outlaws in splendid period piece of such atmosphere you can smell it.

ACT/
ADV

Robin Hood: Prince of Thieves 1991   ★ ★ ★

Kevin Costner's folk hero rather overshadowed by *Alan Rickman's* gloriously hammy Sheriff of Nottingham.

Robocop 1987   ★

Peter Weller as half-man, half-cyborg law-keeper. Distastefully violent but may just be worth watching for special effects.

Rocketeer 1991   ★ ★

Amiable, 1930's spoof in which a unique flying machine brings adventures and danger for pilot hero, *Bill Campbell*.

Rocky 1976   ★ ★ ★

Raw energy emanates from *Sylvester Stallone's* portrayal of small-time fighter given a shot at the title. Best of the series.

Rocky 2 1979   ★

Adequate sequel continues much along lines of original. But by now we've seen it all before.

Rocky 3 1982   ★

And we see it all again as Rocky loses title to Mr T. and goes for the re-match.

Rocky 4 1985   ★

Utter nonsense as Rocky avenges friend's death and fights for World peace against Russian champ, *Dolph Lundgren*.

Rocky 5 1990   ★

Not that you'd notice, but the champ has suffered brain damage; worse, he's lost all his money. Who cares?

Rollerball 1975   ★ ★

James Caan as the star of an ultra-violent sport in a futuristic society where all other violence is banned.

Romancing the Stone 1984   ★ ★ ★ ★

Romantic adventure. Novelist, *Kathleen Turner*, involved with *Michael Douglas* in search for kidnapped sister in S. America. Fast, enjoyable fun.

Rookie, The 1990

Clint Eastwood a veteran cop, *Charlie Sheen* his apprentice partner in feeble thriller.

Salvador 1986

Oliver Stone's powerful, sobering account of experiences of journalist Richard Boyle (*James Wood*) in war-torn El Salvador.

Scarface 1983

Lengthy, violent remake of the old Howard Hawkes' gangster movie, with *Al Pacino* in the Paul Muni role.

Sea Hawk, The 1940

Errol Flynn cuts a dashing blade as Sir Francis Drake. *Flora Robson* plays Elizabeth I. Good, swashbuckling stuff.

Serpico 1973

Al Pacino as an honest cop fighting alone against corruption. Sidney Lumet's gritty, disturbing adaptation of a true story.

Shaft 1971

Richard Roundtree as the black private investigator in racy, Harlem-based action thriller.

Southern Comfort 1981

Intense, survival-of-the-fittest yarn based on National Guardsmen caught in guerilla warfare in Louisiana swamps.

Spartacus 1960

Spectacular story of slave, *Kirk Douglas*, leading a rebellion against Rome. Good support from likes of *Laurence Olivier, Tony Curtis* and *Peter Ustinov*.

Spy who Loved Me, The 1977

One of the best Bond movies pits *Roger Moore* and *Barbara Bach* against indestructible adversary, Jaws.

Stalag 17 1953

Brilliant blend of drama and wit in Billy Wilder's tale of Americans in a German P.O.W. camp.

Sting, The 1973   ★ ★ ★ ★

Paul Newman and _Robert Redford_ plan elaborate ruse to con crooked businessman _Robert Shaw_. Great fun.

Streets of Fire 1984   ★

Prettier to look at than listen to. Rock 'n' roll fantasy with _Michael Pare_ fighting to free girlfriend, _Diane Lane_, from kidnappers.

Suburban Commando 1991   ★ ★

Wrestler _Hulk Hogan_ stars in riotous farce which is much funnier and more satisfying than you'd expect.

Tango & Cash 1989   ★

Mediocre action movie about two policemen, _Kurt Russell_ and _Sylvester Stallone_, at loggerheads over different attitudes to profession.

Terminator, The 1984   ★ ★ ★ ★

Robot, _Arnold Schwarzenegger_, sent back from future to stop mother-to-be, _Sarah Hamilton_, from giving birth to future saviour. Special effects and stunts the real stars.

Terminator 2 1991   ★ ★ ★ ★

Arnie's back - this time as a goody protecting _Hamilton_ and her son from evil Cyborg. Story takes back seat to special effects even better than in the original.

Thelma & Louise 1991   ★ ★ ★ ★ ★

A smashing movie. Great photography, outstanding performances by _Geena Davis_ and _Susan Sarandon_, as two rebellious women having a ball on the run for murder.

This Gun for Hire 1942   ★ ★ ★

Ingenious suspense drama has gunman _Alan Ladd_ out for revenge against double-crosser, helped by _Veronica Lake_.

Three Musketeers, The 1973   ★ ★

Entertaining, tongue-in-cheek version of the romantic swashbuckler with _Oliver Reed_, _Richard Chamberlain_, _Michael York_, _Raquel Welch_, _Charlton Heston_ and _Faye Dunaway_.

Thunderball 1965   ★ ★

Fourth James Bond movie. _Sean Connery_ as 007, _Adolfo Celi_ his adversary. Mixture much as before.

Thunderbolt and Lightfoot 1974

Engaging, moving story of drifter, *Jeff Bridges*, and crook, *Clint Eastwood*, seeking hidden proceeds of old robbery. Bridges particularly good.

To Have and Have Not 1944

A sort of Howard Hawks version of 'Casablanca'. *Humphrey Bogart*, reluctantly embroiled with French resistance while wooing *Lauren Bacall*.

Top Gun 1986

Young naval pilot, *Tom Cruise*, conducts passionate love affair with *Kelly McGillis* against backdrop of incredible flying sequences.

Tora! Tora! Tora! 1970

Tense action movie portraying events leading to attack on Pearl Harbour from both American and Japanese point of view.

Total Recall 1990

Arnold Schwarzenegger provides the brawn, special effects the brain in violent futuristic thriller in which technology can inject memories into minds.

Towering Inferno, The 1974

Contrived disaster movie, enhanced by good effects and expensive cast; *Paul Newman, Steve McQueen, Fred Astaire*, et al..

Treasure of the Sierra Madre 1948

John Huston's classic moral drama of three gold prospectors, *Humphrey Bogart, Walter Huston* and *Tim Holt*, greedily fighting it out down Mexico way.

Twelve o'Clock High 1949

Great performances by *Gregory Peck* and *Dean Jagger* in taut absorbing story of American bomber crews based in England during WWII.

Under Fire 1983

Nick Nolte and *Gene Hackman* as journalists on front line of Nicaraguan rebellion in tense political thriller.

Untouchables, The 1987

Prohibition Chicago's the setting for F.B.I. agent Elliot Ness (*Kevin Costner*) to bring down Al Capone (*Robert De Niro*) with the help of policeman, *Sean Connery*.

ACT/ADV

Viva Zapata! 1952

Marlon Brando outstanding as legendary Mexican revolutionary rising to the Presidency.

Wargames 1983

Computer whizzkid, *Matthew Broderick*, creates enjoyable havoc when he taps into American defence programme.

War Party 1989

History repeats itself when abused, disgruntled, contemporary Red Indians go to war with the Paleface.

Wild at Heart 1990

...and weird on top. Ferocious, funny David Lynch tale of *Nicholas Cage* and *Laura Dern* as bizarre couple on the run.

Wild One, The 1954

The original biker movie, once banned in Britain. Misunderstood *Marlon Brando* and gang run riot in town.

Wings of the Apache 1990

A poor man's 'Top Gun'. Helicopters instead of planes. *Nicholas Cage* and *Sean Young* instead of Tom Cruise and Kelly McGillis.

Year of Living Dangerously, The 1983

Fine performances projected *Mel Gibson* and *Sigourney Weaver* to stardom as a couple investigating political crisis in Indonesia. *Linda Hunt* won Oscar as Gibson's (male) side-kick.

You Only Live Twice 1967

Sean Connery in typical fast, jokey James Bond caper. *Donald Pleasance* as the evil Blofeld.

Zulu 1964

Stanley Baker and *Michael Caine* at Battle of Rourkes's Drift during the Zulu wars. Superb battle scenes.

Addam's Family, The 1991 (on video Summer 92) ★★★

Ghoulish comic strip family brought to life Hollywood-style by *Angelica Huston*, *Raul Julia* and *Christopher Lloyd*.

After Hours 1985 ★★★

Martin Scorcese's likeable offbeat comedy about a night-in-the-life of lonely computer operator, *Griffin Dunne*, in hostile Manhattan.

Airplane! 1980 ★★★★

Hilarious skit on the 'Airport' disaster movies with *Leslie Neilson* and *Lloyd Bridges*.

Airplane II, The Sequel 1982 ★★

Much the same as 'Airplane' only not so good. Notable cameo though from *William Shatner*, a.k.a. Captain Kirk.

Alfie 1966 ★★★

Dated but entertaining 1960's tale of philandering Cockney charmer, *Michael Caine*.

Alice 1991 ★★★

Surreal moral comedy by *Woody Allen*. Rich, bored housewife, *Mia Farrow*, finds the meaning of life from magical Chinese herbs.

All of Me 1984 ★★★

Lily Tomlin shares *Steve Martin's* body in screwball comedy with a fair share of laughs.

Almost an Angel 1990 ★

Soppy, comic fable of soft-hearted crook given second chance at life. Despite *Paul Hogan* the comedy falls flat.

Always 1985 ★★★

Spielberg's charming romance of the old school sees *Richard Dreyfuss* as ghostly guardian angel to old flame, *Holly Hunter*.

American Graffiti 1973 ★★★

Director George Lucas' nostalgic look at '60's U.S.A.. Great rock 'n' roll sound-track and impressive cast.

And Now For Something Completely Different 1972

Collection of Monty Python's TV best including 'The dead parrot' sketch.

Annie Hall 1977

Woody Allen's romantic comedy. He stars as neurotic falling for *Diane Keaton*.

Another You 1991 (on video Summer 92)

Raucus comedy pairing of *Gene Wilder* and *Richard Pryor* as a con-man and chronic liar.

Apartment, The 1960

Jack Lemmon and *Shirley MacLaine* shine in Billy Wilder's sharp comedy/drama.

Arsenic and Old Lace 1944

Cary Grant at his effortless best tries to stop two elderly ladies poisoning lonely old men. Time-honoured classic.

Arthur 1981

Dudley Moore's an unhappy millionaire risking inheritance for the woman, *Liza Minnelli*, he loves. *John Gielgud's* butler steals show.

Article 99 1991 (on video Autumn 92)

Keifer Sutherland and *Ray Liotta* lead this M*A*S*H-style comedy set in Vietnam Vets' hospital.

Baby Boom 1987

Yuppie, hard-nosed business woman, *Diane Keaton*, finds happiness when she inherits a baby.

Bananas 1971

Whacky, slightly uneven caper from *Woody Allen* who finds himself caught up in a S. American revolution.

Barefoot in the Park 1967

Neil Simon's funny, engaging play of struggling, squabbling newly-weds, *Jane Fonda* and *Robert Redford*, buying a fifth floor New York flat.

Barton Fink 1991

Surreal comedy from the Coen brothers about Hollywood, writers block and a serial killer. With *John Turturro* and *John Goodman*.

Beetlejuice 1988

Comic caper of ghosts, *Alec Baldwin* and *Geena Davis*, trying to exorcise modernist family from home with help of whacky Betelgeuse, *Michael Keaton*.

Betsy's Wedding 1990

Alan Alda's mannered comedy revolves around the preparations for daughter's, *Molly Ringwald*, big day.

Beverley Hills Cop 1984

Fast-talking, wise-cracking cop, *Eddie Murphy*, takes L.A. vacation to find friend's killer. Great undemanding stuff.

Big 1988

Tom Hanks gives spirited performance as a twelve-year-old in adult body and world.

Big Picture, The 1989

Engaging satire with *Kevin Bacon* as promising film-maker corrupted by Hollywood.

Bill and Ted's Bogus Journey 1991 (on video Summer 92)

The dudes travel through heaven and hell in amusing sequel notable for jokes and special effects

Bill and Ted's Excellent Adventure 1989

Keanu Reeves and *Alex Winter* as the cool dudes given history lesson via time machine phone box. Lively fun.

Biloxi Blues 1988

Neil Simon's delightful observations of raw recruits in wartime training camp. *Matthew Broderick* stars.

Bird on a Wire 1990

Acceptable action comedy pairs ex-lovers, *Mel Gibson* and *Goldie Hawn*, running from killer.

Blazing Saddles 1974   ★ ★ ★

Mel Brooks' hilarious western spoof with *Gene Wilder*. Noted farting scene after bean supper.

Blues Brothers, The 1980   ★ ★

John Landis cult comedy with *James Belushi* and *Dan Akroyd* as musicians trying to save an orphanage. Great score.

Bob and Carol and Ted and Alice 1969   ★ ★

Two couples with conflicting views of marriage try the others' way in witty social comedy.

Breakfast Club, The 1985   ★ ★

John Hughes comic teen flick set in school detention class. Brat-Pack cast headed by *Emilio Estevez* and *Molly Ringwald*.

Bringing up Baby 1938   ★ ★ ★ ★ ★

Brilliant Howard Hawkes' classic. Inspired pairing of *Cary Grant* and *Katherine Hepburn* brought together by missing leopard.

Broadcast News 1987   ★ ★ ★ ★

Sharp, enjoyable skit on TV journalism with *William Hurt, Holly Hunter* and *Albert Brooks*.

Broadway Danny Rose 1984   ★ ★ ★ ★

Woody Allen as Broadway agent involved with third-rate variety acts and Mafia moll, *Mia Farrow*. Delightful.

Bus Stop 1956   ★ ★

Comedy/drama of a rodeo star, *Don Murray*, pursuing sexy showgirl, *Marilyn Monroe* in one of her best roles.

Butcher's Wife, The 1991   ★ ★

Sporadic laughs in romantic story about a clairvoyant, *Demi Moore*.

Cadillac Man 1990   ★

Car salesman, *Robin Williams*, held hostage by *Tim Robbins* in story that starts well but fades fast.

California Suite 1978

Four separate but intertwined stories of guests at Beverley Hills Hotel. Sharp, funny script by Neil Simon.

Captain's Paradise, The 1953

COM

Comedy with *Alec Guinness* as British sea captain with wife in every port.

Carry on up the Khyber 1968

One of the best of series with typical lavatorial humour and usual cast.

City Lights 1931

Charlie Chaplin's sweet but hugely sentimental classic about his love for blind flower seller.

City Slickers 1991

Witty, charming story in which *Billy Crystal*, *Bruno Kirby* and *Daniel Stern* work out mid-life crisis on modern cattle drive.

Clockwise 1986

Madcap vehicle for *John Cleese*, desperately trying to get to Norwich in time for headmasters' convention.

Comfort and Joy 1984

Bill Forsyth's quirky story of ice cream wars in Glasgow. *Bill Paterson's* splendid as disc jockey who gets involved.

Commitments, The 1991

Alan Parker's funny, joyous story of a Dublin soul band.

Compromising Positions 1985

Housewife *Susan Sarandon* gets involved in lively, amusing murder investigation by detective, *Raul Julia*, when her dentist is killed.

Cook, the Thief, his Wife and her Lover, The 1989 ★ ★ ★ ★

Peter Greenaway's visually astonishing black comedy set in restaurant of greedy gang boss, *Michael Gambon*. Horrifying as well as funny.

Coup de Ville 1990 (on video Summer 92)

Three squabbling brothers ordered by dominant father to drive Cadillac across U.S.A.. Weak comedy, though *Alan Arkin* is excellent.

Cousins 1989

Ted Danson and *Isabella Rossellini* as lovers and cousins in family comedy. Inferior American remake of French 'Cousin, Cousine'.

Crazy People 1990

Dudley Moore finds *Darryl Hannah* and sanity in lunatic asylum. Silly but agreeable.

Crocodile Dundee 1986

Surprisingly but deservedly successful yarn of outback woodsman, *Paul Hogan*, uprooted to Manhattan. Great fun.

Crocodile Dundee 2 1988

More violence, fewer jokes as *Paul Hogan* leaves Manhattan and returns to Oz to trap drug dealers.

Dancin' Thru the Dark 1989

Willy Russell's slice of Liverpudlian life. Hen night and Stag night end up in same disco with disastrous results.

Day at the Races, A 1937

Typical *Marx Brothers* vehicle graced by *Maureen O'Hara*. Perfunctory story; brothers on top form.

Dead Men Don't Wear Plaid 1982

Clever editing sees private eye *Steve Martin* meeting late Hollywood greats in pleasant film noir pastiche.

Desperately Seeking Susan 1985

Excellent comedy of mistaken identities between kooky *Rosanna Arquette* and streetwise *Madonna* in her best film role.

Diner 1982

Thoughtful, funny, inconsequential tale about a group of friends (including *Ellen Barkin* and *Mickey Rourke*) hanging out in a Baltimore café in the late 1950's.

Dinner at Eight 1989

TV remake of 1930's movie. Events leading up to elegant dinner party. *Lauren Bacall* heads excellent cast.

Dirty Rotten Scoundrels 1988

Good knockabout fun with *Steve Martin* and *Michael Caine* as con-men working the French Riviera.

COM

Doc Hollywood 1991

Enchanting comic fairytale of budding plastic surgeon, *Michael J. Fox*, lured from fame and fortune in city job by charm of small town life.

Don't Tell Her it's Me 1990

Shelley Long helps disfigured *Steve Guttenberg* win woman of his dreams in sloppy comedy.

Do the Right Thing 1989

Spike Leigh confronts racial issues in this part-comedy, part-drama slice of life.

Down and Out in Beverley Hills 1986

Comic adventures prompted when tramp, *Nick Nolte*, tries to commit suicide in *Richard Dreyfuss'* and *Bette Midler's* pool.

Dragnet 1987

Amusing parody of TV police shows with *Tom Hanks* and *Dan Akroyd* the hapless cops. Starts better than it finishes.

Dream Team, The 1989

Hilarious adventures of four mental patients at large in downtown New York and solving crime. *Michael Keaton* and *Christopher Lloyd*.

Dr Strangelove 1964   ★ ★ ★ ★

Triple role for *Peter Sellers* in Stanley Kubrick's deep black satire about crazy U.S. General launching nuclear attack on Russia.

Eat the Peach 1986   ★ ★

Engaging account of two unemployed Irish friends who decide to build a wall of death after seeing Elvis movie 'Roustabout'.

Educating Rita 1983

Delightful, touching tale about Liverpudlian hairdresser, *Julie Walters*, taking Open University degree under tutorship of *Michael Caine*.

18 Again! 1988

Aged *George Burns* and grandson swap bodies with feeble results.

Entertaining Mister Sloane 1970

Beryl Reid outstanding in Joe Orton's kinky brother and sister comedy/drama.

Eric the Viking 1989

Monty Python's Terry Jones directed this scrappy, sometimes funny, story of Norsemen setting off to save the world.

Everything You Wanted to Know about Sex (but were afraid to ask) 1972

Woody Allen's hotch-potch series of comic sketches. Very hit and miss.

Every Which Way But Loose 1978

Lightweight comic modern-day western pairing *Clint Eastwood* as gallant clod and orang utan as his smarter companion.

Father of the Bride 1991 (on video Autumn 92)

Steve Martin faces paternal mid-life crisis and vast expense when daughter gets married. Less funny than it should be, but okay.

Filofax 1990

Convict, *James Belushi*, finds *Charles Grodin's* filofax and takes over his life. Has its moments.

Fish Called Wanda, A 1988 ★ ★ ★ ★ ★

Hilarious caper set in England where three robbers, *Jamie Lee Curtis*, *Kevin Kline* and *Michael Palin,* seek help of barrister, *John Cleese,* to find loot.

Fortune Cookie, The 1966 ★ ★

Substandard Billy Wilder comedy in which *Jack Lemmon* and *Walter Matthau* try to pull off an insurance scam.

COM

Foul Play 1978

★ ★

Detective, *Chevy Chase*, falls in love with suspect, *Goldie Hawn*, unwittingly involved in plot to kill Pope.

Frankie and Johnny 1991

★ ★ ★

Gary Marshall's bitter-sweet comedy set in a N.Y. greasy spoon where romance blossoms between lonely hearts, *Michelle Pfeiffer* and *Al Pacino*.

Freshman, The 1991

★ ★ ★

College student, *Matthew Broderick*, falls in with mobster, *Marlon Brando*, gloriously parodying his Godfather role.

General, The 1927

★ ★ ★ ★

Best of *Buster Keaton's* stunt-filled romps, set during the civil war. Keaton in search of his stolen train.

Genevieve 1953

★ ★ ★

Delightful British romp about the rivalry between classic car owners, *Kenneth Moore* and *John Gregson*, during London to Brighton race and after.

Gentlemen Prefer Blondes 1953

★ ★

Harold Hawkes musical comedy provides lightweight show-case for man-hungry *Marilyn Monroe* and *Jane Russell*.

Georgy Girl 1966

★ ★ ★

Frumpy *Lyn Redgrave*, mistress to *James Mason*, with *Charlotte Rampling* as her bitchy friend in swinging sixties comedy.

Ghost 1990

★ ★ ★ ★

Hugely popular comedy/drama sees murdered *Patrick Swayze* returning to protect his threatened lover, *Demi Moore*. *Whoopi Goldberg* as medium lifts tone delightfully.

Ghostbusters 1984

★ ★ ★ ★

Who you gonna call if plagued by ghosts? *Dan Akroyd*, *Harold Ramis* and *Bill Murray*. Rib-tickling comedy with scary special effects.

Ghostbusters II 1989

★ ★ ★

Old gang return with fewer laughs, more violence as they battle a New Year's Eve explosion of spirits.

Gods Must Be Crazy, The 1981

Three stories amalgamate in eccentric slapstick from South Africa which has developed cult following.

Gold Rush, The 1925

The Klondike 1898 provides the setting for *Charlie Chaplin's* silent classic in which he eats his footwear.

Goodbye Girl, The 1977

Touching, funny, love story between lodger, *Richard Dreyfuss,* and divorcee, *Marsha Mason*. Written by Neil Simon.

Green Card 1990

Romantic comedy sees *Gérard Depardieu* and *Andie MacDowell* in a marriage of convenience and a divorce of courtship.

Gregory's Girl 1981

Perceptive direction by Bill Forsyth and an outstanding debut by *John Gordon Sinclair*. A comic jewel.

Hairspray 1988

John Waters' nostalgic, comic satire of the style and fashions of the dance-crazed 1960's.

Hannah and Her Sisters 1986

Woody Allen's best plot to date concentrates on the fortunes of three sisters, *Mia Farrow, Barbara Hershey* and *Dianne Wiest*.

Happy Together 1989

Enthusiastic performances by *Patrick Dempsey* and *Helen Slater* rescue teenage romance plot from banality.

Hard Way, The 1989

Movie star *Michael J. Fox* attaches himself to unwelcoming, hard-nosed N.Y. cop, *James Woods*, to research a forthcoming role.

Harvey 1950

Sheer delight about an endearing drunk, *James Stewart*, whose relatives want him committed because his best friend is an invisible, six-foot rabbit.

Heartbreak Kid, The 1972   ★ ★ ★

Charles Grodin tires of wife on honeymoon where he falls for _Cybil Shepherd_ in poignant, bitter-sweet Neil Simon comedy of embarrassment.

Heart Condition 1990   ★ ★

Racist cop, _Bob Hoskins_, given heart of dead black lawyer, _Denzel Washington_, who returns to haunt him, help him and change him.

Heathers 1989   ★ ★ ★

Christian Slater and _Winona Ryder_ sparkle in this sharp black comedy about adolescence and high school politics.

High Anxiety 1977   ★ ★

Disappointing attempt by _Mel Brooks_ to do to Hitchcock what he'd done to westerns in 'Blazing Saddles.'

High Hopes 1988   ★ ★ ★

Mike Leigh's biting satire of Thatcherite London.

Hobson's Choice 1954   ★ ★ ★ ★

Stirring yet comic performance from _Charles Laughton_ as a conservative father opposed to his daughter's wedding. David Lean directed.

Home Alone 1990   ★ ★ ★

Eight-year old _Macaulay Culkin_, mistakenly left at home alone for Christmas, fights off burglars and discovers the value of family life. Overly sentimental but amusing.

Hooper 1978   ★ ★

Lightweight adventures of aging Hollywood stuntman, _Burt Reynolds_, and his youthful rival.

Hot Shots 1991   ★ ★

Charlie Sheen and _Lloyd Bridges_ attempt to do to 'Top Gun' what 'Airplane' did to 'Airport'. Nice try, doesn't quite work.

How to Get Ahead in Advertising 1989   ★ ★

More satirical than funny comedy about marketing man, _Richard E. Grant_, with a talking boil on his neck.

Hue and Cry 1947

Charming Ealing comedy sees group of youngsters catching gang of crooks. *Alistair Sim* and *Jack Warner* among familiar faces.

I Love You to Death 1990

True, comic story about a wife, *Tracy Ullman*, who botched numerous attempts to murder her cheating husband, *Kevin Kline*.

I'm Alright Jack 1959

Funny spoof on the British work ethic. *Peter Sellers* and *Ian Carmichael* lead excellent cast.

I'm Gonna Git You, Sucka 1988

Hip, witty parody of 1970's Blaxploitation movies.

Importance of Being Ernest, The 1952

Edith Evans' delivery of line 'A handbag!' immortalized this delightful adaptation of Oscar Wilde's play.

Indiscreet 1958

Typically enjoyable *Cary Grant* romantic comedy. *Ingrid Bergman* as the woman he can't forget.

It Happened One Night 1934

Classic romantic Frank Capra comedy. Marvellous pairing of reporter, *Clark Gable*, and runaway heiress, *Claudette Colbert*.

Jabberwocky 1977

Terry Gilliam's hit and miss medieval romp about serfs and a dragon. *Michael Palin* stars.

Jerk, The 1979

Steve Martin in first leading role. Hilariously naive white boy leaves adoptive black family and joins a circus.

Joe Versus the Volcano 1990

Lightweight fantasy about hypochondriac, *Tom Hanks*, conned into making himself human sacrifice. *Meg Ryan* provides romantic interest in three roles.

Jumpin' Jack Flash 1986 ★★★

Whoopi Goldberg as computer operator embroiled in espionage. Neat outlet for her comic flair.

Kentucky Fried Movie 1977 ★★★

Irreverant series of skits and sketches from the creators of 'Airplane'. Vulgar, hilarious and sometimes both.

Kind Hearts and Coronets 1949 ★★★★★

Classic British black comedy in which *Alec Guinness* plays all eight members of a wealthy family being bumped off by ambitious relative.

Kindergarten Cop 1990 ★★

Mean policeman, *Arnold Schwarzenegger*, goes undercover as primary school teacher in a tale too violent to be funny.

King Ralph 1991 ★

Daft farce has Las Vegas cabaret artist, *John Goodman*, ascending to British throne.

Ladykillers, The 1955 ★★★★★

Ealing caper of highest class. Gang of crooks, *Alec Guinness, Peter Sellers* et al., hole up with seemingly innocent old lady.

L. A. Story 1990 ★★

Low-key *Steve Martin* comedy about love and life in smog-ridden city. Some, but not enough, excellent moments.

Lavender Hill Mob, The 1951 ★★★★

Classic Ealing stuff. *Alec Guinness* plans the perfect robbery aided and abetted by *Stanley Holloway* and *Sid James*.

Lenny; Live and Unleashed 1989 ★★★

Lenny Henry's one-man show. Very funny in parts, particularly his take-off of Steve Martin.

Letter to Brezhnev 1985 ★★★

Likeable Liverpudlian comedy about two girls, *Alexandra Pigg* and *Margi Clark*, seeking aid of Soviet president in their romance with Russian sailors.

Life is Sweet 1990

So is this smashing, funny delight from Mike Leigh. A slice of suburban family life which is not to be missed.

Life of Brian 1979

Hugely controversial and achingly funny send-up of organised religion in which Brian is mistaken for the Messiah.

Life Stinks 1991

As does this feeble effort by *Mel Brooks*, who stars as ruthless millionaire experiencing life as a tramp.

Little Shop of Horrors, The 1986

Mixed genres of horror, comedy and musical spark mixed reaction to Frank Oz's movie. *Rick Moranis*, *Steve Martin* and *Bill Murray* among the cast.

Local Hero 1983

Bill Forsyth's delightful examination of effect on Scottish coastal village when American tycoon wants to buy it for oil refinery.

Look Who's Talking 1989

Original comedy of a baby's (voice by *Bruce Willis*) eye view of the world. *Kirsty Alley* as mother, *John Travolta* as baby sitter.

Look Who's Talking Too 1990

Baby Mikey gets a sister (voiced by *Roseanne Barr*) in witless, uncharming sequel.

Love and Death 1975

One of *Woody Allen's* best. Sharp skit on Russian literature and various movies. *Diane Keaton* co-stars.

Love at First Bite 1979

Pleasing spoof of Dracula movies with *George Hamilton* as suave C20th count with a lust for blood.

Madhouse 1990

Silly family farce about guests who never leave redeemed somewhat by presence of *Kirstie Alley*.

Maid The 1990

Businessman, *Martin Sheen*, becomes *Jacqueline Bisset's* maid in order to woo her. Lightweight romantic comedy.

Major League 1989

Bitchy woman owner plots downfall of already no-hoper baseball team. Players, *Tom Berenger* and *Charlie Sheen* etc., out to thwart her.

Manhattan 1979

Woody Allen's satirical black and white comedy of life and love in New York. *Diane Keaton* and *Mariel Hemingway* the objects of Allen's desire.

Man in the White Suit, The 1951

Alec Guinness as scientist who's invented everlasting cloth. Big business wants formula destroyed in delightful Ealing comedy.

Man with Two Brains, The 1983

Steve Martin's funniest comedy. He plays a brilliant brain surgeon seduced by conniving vamp, *Kathleen Turner*.

Married to It 1991 (on video Autumn 92)

Mediocre comedy about married life in New York with *Cybil Shepherd* and *Ron Silver*.

Married to the Mob 1988

Enjoyable comic adventure of gangster's moll, *Michelle Pfeiffer*, trying to cut ties from the mob. *Matthew Modine* her police protector.

M*A*S*H 1970

This scathing story of a U.S. military medical unit in Korean war spawned long running TV series. *Donald Sutherland* and *Elliott Gould*, the charismatic doctors.

Meaning of Life, The 1983

Monty Python's irreverent, uneven series of sketches exploring various facets of life and death. Occasionally hilarious.

Meet the Applegates 1991

Insects in human guise plot to end the world in weak but inoffensive fable.

Mermaids 1990

Terrific little comedy featuring *Cher* as single mother unable to settle. *Winona Ryder, Bob Hoskins* and sound-track provide great support.

Micki and Maude 1984

Dudley Moore amusing as bigamist trying to placate his two wives, *Amy Irving* and *Ann Reinking*.

Midnight Run 1988

Comedy/action adventure matches bounty hunter, *Robert De Niro*, against fugitive, *Charles Grodin*, whose performance steals film.

Midsummer Night's Sex Comedy, A 1982

Woody Allen's wryly amusing look at sexual interaction of three couples on weekend holiday.

Miss Firecracker 1989

Low-key comedy of Mississippi small-town life. *Holly Hunter* very good as lonely girl seeking love and self esteem.

Missionary, The 1982

Easy-going comedy with *Michael Palin* as minister helping fallen women in Victorian London.

Monty Python and the Holy Grail 1973

Comic crew's wickedly funny send-up of the Arthurian legend.

Moonstruck 1987 ★ ★ ★ ★ ★

Enchanting romantic comedy set in Little Italy where Cher falls in love with fiancée's brother, *Nicholas Cage*.

Mr. Deeds Goes to Town 1936 ★ ★ ★ ★

Frank Capra comedy wherein *Gary Cooper* inherits fortune and finds his sanity disputed when he tries to give it away.

Murder by Death 1976

Neil Simon's spoof of murder mysteries provides passable comic vehicle for *Peter Sellers, Maggie Smith* and *David Niven*.

My Blue Heaven 1990   ★ ★

Fairly amusing story of mobster, *Steve Martin*, who goes into witness protection programme with help of F.B.I agent, *Rick Moranis*.

My Cousin Vinny 1992 (on video Winter 92)   ★ ★

COM

Courtroom comedy with *Joe Pesci* as inept lawyer defending cousin, *Ralph Macchio*, on murder charge.

My Favourite Wife 1940   ★ ★ ★

Presumed widower, *Cary Grant*, all set to remarry when his lost wife, *Irene Dunne*, comes back. Pleasing fun.

My Favourite Year 1982   ★ ★ ★ ★

Peter O'Toole walks off with this funny, touching tale of a boozy, has-been actor making come-back on live TV show.

My Stepmother is an Alien 1988   ★ ★

Scientist, *Dan Aykroyd,* involved in comic capers when he marries extra-terrestrial, *Kim Bassinger*.

Mystery Date 1991 (on video Summer 92)   ★

Inexperienced youngster, *Ethan Hawke*, finds himself on a blind date with an older woman, *Teri Polo*.

Naked Gun, The 1988   ★ ★ ★ ★

Hilarious police spoof starring *Leslie Neilsen* and *Priscilla Presley*. By the makers of 'Airplane!'.

Naked Gun 2 1/2 1991   ★ ★ ★

Nearly as funny as original. *Leslie Neilsen's* back to save the world from toxic waste, aided and abetted by *Presley*.

National Health, The 1973   ★ ★

Jim Dale and *Lynn Redgrave* star in acerbic black comedy about the British health service.

National Lampoon's Animal House 1978   ★ ★

Sex, drugs and rock 'n' roll are the targets of hit-and-miss American college farce with *John Belushi*.

Necessary Roughness 1991 (on video Autumn 92)   ★

Farmer, *Scott Bakula*, goes to college to save its football team. Predictable and feeble comedy.

Night at the Opera, A 1935   ★ ★ ★

Possibly best-loved film from *Marx Brothers*, though 'Duck Soup' is better.

Night to Remember, A 1943   ★ ★ ★

Mystery writer and wife, *Brian Aherne* and *Loretta Young*, investigate murder in lively comedy/thriller.

9 to 5 1980   ★ ★

Cast, *Jane Fonda*, *Lily Tomlin* and *Dolly Parton*, better than plot in office-based satire.

Ninotchka 1939   ★ ★ ★ ★

Garbo's most joyous performance as hard-nosed Russian envoy succumbing to love and lure of capitalism.

No Surrender 1985   ★ ★ ★

Biting social satire set in Northern nightclub where two sets of rival old folks come into conflict.

Nuns on the Run 1990   ★ ★ ★

Pleasing British farce with *Robbie Coltrane* and *Eric Idle* posing as nuns to avoid hitmen.

Nuts in May 1984   ★ ★ ★ ★ ★

Hilarious, slice-of-life comedy by Mike Leigh about a right-on, 'green' couple taking a camping holiday.

One, Two, Three 1961   ★ ★ ★

American executive in West Berlin in trouble when boss's daughter marries Communist. Billy Wilder comedy; *James Cagney's* last starring role.

Only the Lonely 1991   ★

Thin comedy about shy policeman, *John Candy*, falling for undertaker's daughter, *Alley Sheedy*, despite mother's disapproval.

Oscar 1991 ★ ★

Farcical plot revolving around marriage plans of mafiosa boss's daughter. *Sylvester Stallone* reveals surprisingly light touch.

Other People's Money 1991 ★ ★ ★

COM

Ruthless Wall Street tycoon, *Danny DeVito*, defied by honourable, old-fashioned *Gregory Peck*. Fast and amusing.

Outrageous Fortune 1987 ★ ★ ★

Ill-matched *Bette Midler* and *Shelley Long* join forces to find the man who deceived them both, in agreeable, raucous adventure.

Overboard 1987 ★ ★

Amnesia causes heiress, *Goldie Hawn*, to rough it as housekeeper to rough *Kurt Russell* and his kids in light romantic comedy.

Owl and the Pussycat, The 1970 ★ ★ ★

Barbara Streisand and *George Segal* charm as incongruous couple; she a prostitute, he a learned bookkeeper.

Parenthood 1989 ★ ★ ★

Touching, funny insights into problems of parenthood in one large family. *Steve Martin* heads splendid cast.

Passport to Pimlico 1949 ★ ★ ★ ★

Wonderful Ealing comedy in which Pimlico declares independence when an ancient Royal Charter is unearthed.

Peggy Sue Got Married 1986 ★ ★

'Back To The Future' yarn. Disillusioned *Kathleen Turner*, given chance to return to high school and change her life.

Personal Services 1987 ★ ★

Exploits of notorious London brothel-keeper, Cynthia Payne (*Julie Walters*). Nice study of British sexual mores.

Pink Panther, The 1964 ★ ★ ★

David Niven the suave cat-burglar pursued by bungling sûreté Inspector Clouseau. *Peter Sellers* hilarious as inept copper.

Planes, Trains and Automobiles 1987

Surprisingly unfunny comedy of problems encountered by *Steve Martin* trying to get home for Thanksgiving. *John Candy* does little to help.

Play it Again, Sam 1972

Woody Allen on top form as writer coached by ghost of Humphrey Bogart in efforts to win *Diane Keaton*.

Plaza Suite 1971

Three funny Neil Simon playlets all linked by same suite in New York's Plaza Hotel.

Police Academy 1984

Farcical romp set in police training camp where misfit recruits need licking into shape.

Pope Must Die, The 1991

Up-and-down comedy of errors. *Robbie Coltrane* mistakenly appointed head of Vatican.

Porky's 1981

Teenage hormones create havoc in 1950's school camp, but rarely raise a laugh.

Pretty Woman 1990

Irresistable fairytale of hooker, *Julia Roberts*, falling in love with wealthy businessman client, *Richard Gere*.

Private Function, A 1985

Funny, sometimes cruel, comedy set in food-rationed, post-war England with *Michael Palin* and *Maggie Smith*.

Private's Progress 1956

Good humoured army farce with *Ian Carmichael*, the national serviceman duped by thieves. *Terry Thomas* and *Richard Attenborough* in support.

Purple Rose of Cairo, The 1985

Delightful *Woody Allen* comedy with *Mia Farrow* as down-trodden housewife whose hero, *Jeff Daniels*, steps out of movie screen and sweeps her away.

Quick Change 1990   ★ ★

The bank raid's easy. It's getting out of N.Y. that bothers _Bill Murray_ and gang, and provides the fun.

Rachel Papers, The 1989   ★

Maladroit attempt at modern comedy of manners based on Martin Amis novel.

Radio Days 1987   ★ ★ ★ ★

Woody Allen's nostalgic, always amusing, reminiscences of boyhood in 1950's Queens, N.Y..

Raising Arizona 1987   ★ ★

Childless couple, _Nicholas Cage_ and _Holly Hunter_, plan to steal one of quintuplets. Untidy comedy. Pre-credit sequence best.

Repossessed 1990   ★ ★

Hit and miss spoof of 'The Exorcist' with _Leslie Neilsen_ driving out the devil; _Linda Blair_ reprising her original role.

Reuben, Reuben 1983   ★ ★

Anarchic comedy of dissolute writer, _Tom Conti_, sponging off married woman until he meets young nurse, _Kelly McGillis_.

Richard Pryor Live in Concert 1982   ★ ★ ★

Some achingly funny stuff taken from the comic's stand-up show.

Riff Raff 1991   ★ ★ ★ ★

Ken Loach's funny, biting satire of Britain under the Tories, set on a building site.

Risky Business 1983   ★ ★ ★

Teenager, _Tom Cruise_, turns absent parents' home into a brothel in imaginative coming-of-age comedy.

Road to Utopia 1945   ★ ★

Fourth of the _Bob Hope, Bing Crosby_ 'road' movies, finds the boys cavorting around Alaska in search of _Dorothy Lamour's_ goldmine.

Room Service 1938

Marx Brothers as destitute producers holed up in hotel room. Not one of their best.

Rosalie Goes Shopping 1989

Comic satire on consumerism. *Marianne Sagebrecht* a bored housewife who mounts up huge shopping bills on credit cards.

Rosencrantz And Guildenstern Are Dead 1990

Tom Stoppard directs lively screen version of his own play. *Tim Roth* and *Gary Oldman* as hapless, untrustworthy and ill-fated friends.

Roxanne 1987

Steve Martin's funny, modern-day version of Cyrano De Bergerac set around a fire station. *Darryl Hannah* as the latter-day Roxanne.

Ruthless People 1986

Bette Midler's so spoiled that when she's kidnapped her husband, *Danny DeVito*, refuses to pay the ransom. Fine comic performance by Midler.

Scenes from a Mall 1991

Disappointing Paul Mazursky comedy starring *Woody Allen*, in which an anniversary shopping trip brings out startling marital revelations between Allen and wife, *Bette Midler*.

Scrooged 1988

Contemporary, comic version of Dickens' 'A Christmas Carol'. *Bill Murray* finds festive spirit with the help of three hip ghosts. Not great, not terrible.

Secret Life of Walter Mitty, The 1947

Whimsical charmer with *Danny Kaye* as the timid Mitty (based on James Thurber character) who day dreams of being a hero. *Virginia Mayo* as love interest.

Seven Year Itch, The 1955

Tom Ewell the middle-aged man attracted, during his wife's absence, to the blonde upstairs, *Marilyn Monroe*. Lovely Billy Wilder comedy, notable for the famous skirt-lifting scene.

Shirley Valentine 1989

Delightful, gentle Willy Russell story. *Pauline Collins* the bored Liverpudlian housewife who ups to a Greek island in search of romance.

Sibling Rivalry 1990　　　　　　　

Nice comic idea, shame about the script. Repressed housewife, *Kirsty Alley*, has brief affair with stranger who, not only dies, but turns out to be her husband's long lost brother.

Slap Shot 1977　　　　　　　

Quick-fire comedy of minor league Ice Hockey team which, under direction of coach/player, *Paul Newman*, learns to play dirty and start winning.

Sleeper 1973　　　　　　　

Sharp humour from *Woody Allen*. He awakens 200 years later in a future where alcohol and smoking are good for you.

Smokey and the Bandit 1977　　　　　　　

Slapstick series of car-chases for trucker, *Burt Reynolds*, in a lightweight comedy but the stunts are fun.

Soapdish 1991　　　　　　　

Off-beat comedy following the off-camera lives of a soap opera cast, including *Sally Field* and *Kevin Kline*.

Some Like it Hot 1959　　　　　　　

Billy Wilder classic. *Jack Lemmon* and *Tony Curtis* pose as members of *Marilyn Monroe's* all-female band to escape gangsters.

Splash 1984　　　　　　　

Humorous fairytale set in modern-day where *Tom Hanks* unknowingly falls in love with a mermaid, *Darryl Hannah*.

Stardust Memories 1980　　　　　　　

Woody Allen's black and white pastiche of Fellini's '8½'. Rather embittered attempt at comedy.

Suburban Commando 1991　　　　　　　★ ★

Wrestler *Hulk Hogan* stars in riotous farce which is much funnier and more satisfying than you'd expect.

Sunshine Boys, The 1975　　　　　　　★ ★ ★ ★

Hilarious Neil Simon comedy of an aging, sparring showbiz duo, *Walter Matthau* and *George Burns*, reunited reluctantly for a big TV show.

Super, The 1991 (on video Autumn 92)   ★ ★

Joe Pesci stars in comedy about landlord forced to live in one of his own slums.

Supergrass, The 1985   ★ ★ ★

Amusing story of smuggling at the seaside from 'The Comic Strip Presents...' team with all the regulars. *Robbie Coltrane, Ade Edmondson*, etc..

Sure Thing, The 1985   ★ ★ ★

Rob Reiner's deft direction of *John Cusack* and *Daphne Zuniga* as two young college students sharing an amusing, adventure-strewn, love-torn ride home.

Talk of the Town, The 1942   ★ ★ ★ ★ ★

Great romantic comedy. *Cary Grant* an escaped convict hiding out in *Jean Arthur's* home, rented by Supreme Court judge, *Ronald Colman*.

Tall Guy, The 1989   ★ ★

Jeff Goldblum plays the fall-guy to *Rowan Atkinson's* comic until he meets nurse, *Emma Thompson*. Pleasing movie, not as good as it should have been.

Taming of the Shrew, The 1967   ★ ★ ★

Franco Zeffirelli's zesty, colourful version of Shakespeare's comedy featuring *Elizabeth Taylor* and *Richard Burton*.

"10" 1979   ★ ★

Male menopause hits Dudley Moore in pretty good comedy co-starring a disrobed *Bo Derek* and *Julie Andrews*.

That Sinking Feeling 1979   ★ ★ ★

Rollicking Bill Forsyth film about a group of young unemployed Glaswegians turning to crime unsuccessfully.

Things Change 1988   ★ ★ ★

Shoe-shiner, *Don Ameche*, agrees to take the rap for a Mafia killer. As a reward, *Joe Montegna* takes him on a lavish fling before he gives himself up.

This is Spinal Tap 1984   ★ ★ ★

Wicked parody of rock-bands and music documentaries. Narrated and directed by Rob Reiner.

Three Men and a Baby 1987   ★ ★ ★

Lively comedy about three confirmed bachelors, *Ted Danson*, *Steve Guttenberg* and *Tom Selleck*, whose lives are disrupted when a baby girl is left on their doorstep.

Three Men and a Little Lady 1990   ★

Crass sequel sees the boys trying to stop young Mary being taken to England by her mother, *Nancy Travis*.

Throw Momma from the Train 1987   ★ ★

Thin comedy in which *Danny DeVito* and *Billy Crystal* exchange murders. (Hitchcock did it straight and much better with 'Strangers On a Train').

Time Bandits, The 1981   ★ ★ ★ ★

Ralph Richardson and six dwarfs escort young boy through time in hilarious romp with a cast of glittering guest stars. *Ian Holm* marvellous as tiny Napoleon.

Tin Men 1987   ★ ★ ★

Danny DeVito and *Richard Dreyfuss* paired as loser and hustler, brought together by a car crash in warmly amusing tale.

Titfield Thunderbolt, The 1953   ★ ★ ★

Unadulterated fun from Ealing. Group of villagers led by *Stanley Holloway* and *Sid James*, fighting to keep their beloved railway.

To Be or Not to Be 1942   ★ ★ ★ ★

Jack Benny and *Carole Lombard* lead this delightful Ernst Lubitsch farce of a group of actors posing as Nazis in war-torn Poland. Glorious bad taste.

Tom Jones 1963   ★ ★ ★

Sprightly version of Henry Fielding's C18th novel about a young man's, *Albert Finney*, bawdy experiences.

Too Hot to Handle 1991   ★ ★

Alec Baldwin and *Kim Bassinger* ooze sex as the star-crossed lovers in this romantic comedy set in 1950's.

Tootsie 1982   ★ ★ ★ ★

Outstanding performance by *Dustin Hoffman* as an actor who passes himself off as a woman in order to get work. Sparkling comedy.

Torch Song Trilogy 1988

Evocative and emotional comedy/drama told in three parts about a homosexual, *Harvey Fierstein*, coming to terms with his problems.

Trading Places 1983

Down-and-out, *Eddie Murphy*, and spoilt rich kid, *Dan Akroyd*, manipulated into swapping lives. Great fun, marred by soppy climax on train.

Trouble with Harry, The 1955

Off-beat Hitchcock comedy/thriller about problems of disposing of a corpse. Stars *John Forsyth* before his hair turned blue in 'Dynasty'.

True Identity 1991

Lenny Henry as actor on wrong side of mob. Great make-up and nice humour.

Turner and Hooch 1989

Entertaining comedy/thriller concerning one cop, *Tom Hanks*, and his dog.

Turtle Diary 1985

Gently amusing fable of repressed couple, *Ben Kingsley* and *Glenda Jackson*, brought together by desire to free giant turtles from the zoo.

Twins 1988

Reasonably comic adventures ensue when unlikely twins, *Danny DeVito* and *Arnold Schwarzenegger*, - separated at birth - are reunited.

Uncle Buck 1989

John Candy, the slobbish relative of the title, baby sitting his brother's brattish kids. Feeble comedy of little substance.

Vice Versa 1988

Judge Reinhold and son, *Fred Savage*, swap bodies in thin, but well-played, role-reversal comedy.

War of the Roses, The 1989 ★ ★ ★ ★

Achingly funny black comedy about marriage turning sour. *Kathleen Turner* and *Michael Douglas* as warring partners.

Weekend at Bernie's 1989   ★

Two lads in fairly amusing trouble when trying to pretend their dead host is still alive and well.

Welcome Home, Roxy Carmichael 1990   ★ ★ ★

Enigmatic comedy about lonely young girl, *Wynona Ryder*, adapting to adoption and relationships.

We're No Angels 1989   ★

Robert De Niro and *Sean Penn* look uncomfortable as escaped convicts passing as priests in feeble comic remake.

What About Bob? 1991   ★ ★ ★

Psychiatrist, *Richard Dreyfuss*, driven mad when his patient, *Bill Murray*, follows him on a family holiday.

What's up Doc? 1972   ★ ★ ★ ★

Great comedy of errors based on a mix-up of mismatched couples. *Ryan O'Neal* and *Barbara Streisand* lead.

When Harry Met Sally 1989   ★ ★ ★ ★

Billy Crystal and *Meg Ryan* put paid to the theory that men and women can have a platonic relationship in delightful tale, featuring THAT fake orgasm scene.

Whisky Galore 1949   ★ ★ ★ ★

Rich Ealing comedy about a small Scottish community stealing cache of whisky from wartime shipwreck.

Who Framed Roger Rabbit? 1988   ★ ★ ★ ★

Outstanding animation combined with live action marks comic caper of detective, *Bob Hoskins*, out to clear the name of wrongly accused rabbit.

Wilt 1988   ★ ★

A blow-up doll causes comic problems for detective *Mel Smith* and murder suspect, *Griff Rhys-Jones*.

Wish You Were Here 1987   ★ ★ ★

British seaside comedy concentrating on the wartime exploits of foul-mouthed young girl, *Emily Lloyd*.

Witches of Eastwick, The 1987 ★ ★ ★

Three beautiful women; *Cher, Susan Sarandon* and *Michelle Pfeiffer* seduced by the devilish *Jack Nicholson*. Good fun.

Withnail and I 1987 ★

1960's based British comedy. Unemployed actors, *Richard E. Grant* and *Paul McGann*, leave life of drink and drugs for disastrous country holiday.

Without a Clue 1988 ★ ★

Sherlock Holmes send-up. Holmes (*Michael Caine*) is really a drunken actor fronting for true genius Doctor Watson (*Ben Kingsley*).

Working Girl 1988 ★ ★ ★ ★

Sophisticated comedy of errors. *Melanie Griffiths* the upwardly-mobile secretary, *Sigourney Weaver* her ruthless boss. *Harrison Ford* provides the love interest.

Young Frankenstein 1974 ★ ★ ★

Funny, farcical parody of Hollywood horror movies by Mel Brooks. *Gene Wilder* the mad scientist, *Madeline Kahn* his fiancée who becomes the monster's wife.

Zelig 1983 ★ ★ ★

Woody Allen as ubiquitous human chameleon who hob-nobs with Hitler and others. Great editing and marvellous trick photography.

Accident 1967

In-depth character study based on Oxford professor, *Dirk Bogarde*, who falls for one of his students.

Accidental Tourist, The 1988

William Hurt plays a travel writer, whose emotional journey through divorce makes for bleak drama lightened by *Geena Davis'* comic touches.

Accused, The 1988 **DRA**

Brilliantly executed rape drama. Victim, Oscar-winner *Jodie Foster*, and lawyer, *Kelly McGillis*, fight for justice.

Agnes of God 1985

Psychiatrist, *Jane Fonda*, is called to Convent where a nun's suspected of murdering her baby.

Airport 1970

First and best of long-running disaster-in-the-sky series. Ruined if you've seen 'Airplane'.

All about Eve 1950

A volatile actress, *Bette Davis*, fastens her seat-belt for a bumpy ride when she befriends *Anne Baxter's* insinuating Eve. Brilliant drama of the old school

All the President's Men 1976

Compelling account of how Washington Post journalists, *Dustin Hoffman* and *Robert Redford*, exposed the Watergate scandal.

All This and Heaven Too 1940

Ill-fated romance between nobleman, *Charles Boyer*, and governess, *Bette Davis*. Weepy melodrama.

American Friends 1991 ★ ★

Michael Palin's gentle, affectionate re-telling of how his great grandfather found true love.

And Justice for All 1979 ★ ★

Behind the scenes shenanigans of the Maryland justice system is a confused show-case for *Al Pacino's* talents.

Anna Karenina 1935

Vivien Leigh in sentimental tale of married woman in love with Russian soldier.

Another Country 1984

Beautiful rendition of spy Guy Burgess' boyhood. *Rupert Everett* and *Colin Firth* excel.

Apprenticeship of Duddy Kravitz, The 1974

Richard Dreyfuss as Jewish lad rising from the Ghettos in this comic drama.

Atlantic City 1944

Louis Malle's wickedly observed character study of winners and losers in a gambling American resort. Probably *Burt Lancaster's* best performance.

Aunt Julia and the Scriptwriter 1991

Budding radio writer, *Keanu Reeves*, falls for his aunt, *Barbara Hershey*, in 1950's New Orleans. *Peter Falk* takes the acting honours.

Avalon 1990

Despite star-studded cast this story of family of Russian Jewish immigrants to America tends to drag.

Awakenings, The 1990

Outstanding performances mark this traumatic tale of a doctor, *Robin Williams*, helping encephalitic patients, *Robert De Niro* amongst others.

Baby It's You 1983

Bittersweet story of high school kids in 1960's New Jersey with *Rosanna Arquette*.

Badlands 1973

Disturbing account of the Starkweather - Fugate spate of killings in 1950's led by *Martin Sheen* and *Sissy Spacek*.

Bad Timing 1980

Nick Roeg's eclectic psychodrama of a Vienna-based affair between attempted suicide, *Theresa Russell*, and her psychoanalyst, *Art Garfunkel*.

Barry Lyndon 1975   ★ ★ ★

Breathtaking photography in Stanley Kubrick's lengthy version of Thackerey's story of an C18th Irish rogue, *Ryan O'Neal*.

Beaches 1988   ★

Unashamedly sentimental tale of love and loss between childhood friends *Bette Midler* and *Barbara Hershey*.

Belly of an Architect, The 1987   ★ ★

Peter Greenaway's great to look at but pretentious tale of dying architect, *Brian Dennehey*, in Rome.

Betrayed 1988   ★ ★ ★

F.B.I. agent, *Debra Winger*, romantically involved with *Tom Berenger*. Love blurs her judgement in investigation of K.K.K. activities.

Big Blue, The 1988   ★

Water-logged tale of insurance investigator, *Rosanna Arquette*, trailing boyfriend around diving competitions.

Big Chill, The 1983   ★ ★ ★ ★

Intelligent direction by Laurence Kasdan of college friends reuniting in mid-life. With *Tom Berenger, Glenn Close, Jeff Goldblum* and *William Hurt*.

Billy Liar 1963   ★ ★ ★

Tom Courtenay plays a day dreamer escaping from dreary life in poignant British film.

Birdy 1984   ★ ★ ★ ★

Vietnam-traumatized Matthew Modine yearns to fly, *Nicholas Cage* determined to help him in thoughtful Alan Parker drama.

Blaze 1989   ★

Promising but disappointing account of a Governor, *Paul Newman*, and his fateful affair with stripper, *Lolita Davidovitch*. Based on real life.

Blood and Sand 1991   ★

Poor boy finds fame, sex and riches as matador in thin remake of Valentino silent pic.

Born on the Fourth of July 1989

Tom Cruise superb as embittered, crippled army vet in Oliver Stone's Vietnam movie.

Boyz N the Hood 1991

Black teenagers struggle to survive in drug-ridden city. Notable debut by director John Singleton.

Breaker Morant 1979

Three Australian soldiers court-martialled for Boer war atrocities. With *Edward Woodward* and *Jack Thompson*.

Breakfast at Tiffanys 1961

Touching love story involving cute call-girl, *Audrey Hepburn*, and writer, *George Peppard*. Good score.

Brian's Song 1970

Warming tale of friendship in face of adversity and rivalry between American footballers *James Caan* and *Billy Dee Williams*.

Brideshead Revisited 1981

Outstanding TV adaptation of Evelyn Waugh's novel. Cast - *Anthony Andrews, Jeremy Irons* etc..- as lavish as sets.

Brief Encounter 1945

Dated but still charming doomed love affair between *Trevor Howard* and *Celia Johnson*.

Bright Angel 1991 (on video Summer 92)

Teenager *Lili Taylor* leaves home and finds trouble.

Broadcast News 1987   ★ ★ ★ ★

Sharp, enjoyable skit on TV journalism with *William Hurt, Holly Hunter* and *Albert Brooks*.

Bugsy 1991 (on video Autumn 92)   ★ ★ ★

Warren Beatty plays the hood who 'invented' Las Vegas as gambling resort. Overlong but good performances.

Bull Durham 1988   ★ ★ ★ ★

Kevin Costner and *Susan Sarandon* nurture the talents of promising baseballer *Tim Robbins*. Neat underrated story.

Buster 1988   ★ ★

Phil Collins more than adequately portrays the Great Train Robber but *Julie Walters* shines as wife.

Caine Mutiny, The 1954   ★ ★ ★

Two Naval officers court-martialled for mutiny against paranoid captain. *Humphrey Bogart* leads excellent cast.

Cal 1984   ★ ★ ★ ★

Exceptional drama of an Irish teenager, *John Lynch*, trying to sever ties with I.R.A..

Candidate, The 1972   ★ ★

Shrewd political satire with *Robert Redford* running for the Senate on ticket of total integrity.

Carnal Knowledge 1971   ★ ★ ★

Jack Nicholson and *Art Garfunkel* change attitudes and sexual hang-ups as they mature from college to middle age.

Casablanca 1942   ★ ★ ★ ★ ★

Classic WWII romance set in Morocco with *Humphrey Bogart* and *Ingrid Bergman*.

Catch 22 1970   ★ ★ ★

Alan Arkin leads good cast in Mike Nichols' honourable attempt to bring Joseph Heller's brilliant anti-war novel to life.

Cat on a Hot Tin Roof 1958   ★ ★ ★

Sparring couple, *Elizabeth Taylor* and *Paul Newman*, in goodish adaptation of Tennessee Williams' scorching melodrama.

Chariots of Fire 1981   ★ ★ ★ ★

Oscar-winning and absorbing story of two British sprinters and their bid for gold medals in 1924 Olympics.

Children of a Lesser God 1986

Touching love affair between teacher, _William Hurt_, and deaf student, _Marlee Matlin_.

Christmas Carol, A 1984

Prettily restaged version of Dickens tale. _George C. Scott_ as Scrooge.

Citizen Kane 1941

One of the best films ever made. Everyone should see it.

City of Joy 1991 (on video Winter 92)

Calcutta slums form setting of intelligent drama with _Patrick Swayze_ and _Pauline Collins_.

Clean and Sober 1988

Tough examination of drug and booze addiction enhanced by _Michael Keaton's_ performance.

Close My Eyes 1991

Sibling incest forms basis of unusual English drama lightened by presence of _Alan Rickman_.

Cocktail 1988

Tom Cruise tends bar and services women. One for Cruise fans only.

Colditz Story, The 1957 ★ ★ ★

British P.O.W.s plan to prove that 'escape proof' German castle is anything but, in ever-popular wartime escape saga.

Color of Money 1986 ★ ★

So-so sequel to 'The Hustler' pairs sex symbols _Tom Cruise_ and _Paul Newman_ in battle of green baize. Oscar for _Newman_.

Color Purple, The 1985 ★ ★

Spielberg's over-lavish, unconvincing story of young black woman's hard life and times in American south. _Whoopi Goldberg_ stars.

Come See the Paradise 1990   ★ ★

Alan Parker's worthy exposé of persecution of Japanese Americans in U.S.A. during WWII. *Dennis Quaid* leads.

Coming Home 1978   ★ ★

Trauma of crippled Vietnam veteran and effect of war on those back home. Oscars for *Jane Fonda* and *Jon Voight*.

Connection, The 1961   ★ ★ ★   DRA

Tough drama of documentary director filming a group of junkies awaiting their next fix.

Cook, the Thief, his Wife and her Lover, The 1989   ★ ★ ★ ★

Peter Greenaway's visually astonishing black comedy set in restaurant of greedy gang boss, *Michael Gambon*. Horrifying as well as funny.

Cool Hand Luke 1967   ★ ★ ★ ★

Convict *Paul Newman* as individual fighting penal system. Similar in theme (and compares very favourably) to 'One Flew Over the Cuckoo's Nest'.

Crimes and Misdemeanours 1989   ★ ★ ★

Woody Allen's bold, skillful blending and bringing together of two separate stories involving comedy, murder and adultery.

Criminal Justice 1990   ★

Courtroom drama notable for *Forest Whitaker's* performance as black defendant accused of mugging unsavoury young woman.

Criss Cross 1991 (on video Winter 92)   ★

Goldie Hawn as single mother forced to take job stripping.

Crossing Delancey 1988   ★ ★

Charming, wistful tale of romance and arranged marriage in Jewish community in downtown New York.

Cry Freedom 1987   ★ ★ ★

Richard Attenborough's fiercely anti-apartheid drama of friendship between South African journalist, Donald Woods, and black activist, Steve Biko.

Cry in the Dark 1988

Based on the 'Dingo baby' case in Australia. *Meryl Streep* exceptional as woman accused of infanticide.

Dad 1989

Slushy father and son reconciliation drama. *Jack Lemmon* seriously miscast as irascible father to *Ted Danson*.

Dance with a Stranger 1985

Fine British reconstruction of events leading to hanging of Ruth Ellis (*Miranda Richardson*) for murder. *Rupert Everett* supports.

Dangerous Liaisons 1988

Sexual games and corruption in C18th France. *Glenn Close, John Malkovitch* and *Michelle Pfeiffer*. Grippingly told.

Dark Victory 1939

Dying *Bette Davis* falls in love with doctor in weepy melodrama. *Davis* on top form. *Humphrey Bogart* curiously miscast.

David Copperfield 1935

M.G.M.'s version of Dickens' novel. *W.C.Fields* hilarious as Mr. McCawber.

Days of Heaven 1978

Turn of the century ménage-à-trois among immigrants in mid-west, with *Richard Gere* and *Brooke Shields*.

Dead, The 1987

Superb adaptation by John Huston (his last film) of James Joyce story. *Angelica Huston* and terrific Irish cast.

Dead Poets Society 1989 ★ ★ ★ ★

Peter Weir's moving, thoughtful drama about unorthodox teacher *Robin Williams* and his effect on his pupils.

Death in Venice 1971 ★ ★ ★

Visconti's slow, beautiful version of Thomas Mann novel with *Dirk Bogarde* as dying artist obsessed with young boy.

Deer Hunter, The 1978

★ ★ ★ ★

Powerful, painful story of young Pittsburgh workers before, during and after Vietnam war. *Robert De Niro* and *Meryl Streep*.

Deliverance 1972

★ ★ ★ ★

Horrifying events overtake *Burt Reynolds* and friends on canoe trip through hill-billy country. Probably *Reynolds'* best performance.

Devils, The 1970

★ ★

C17th nuns apparently possessed by devil. Ken Russell's once controversial, sexy shocker.

Distant Voices, Still Lives 1988

★ ★ ★

Haunting, stylized memories of a working class family and its births, deaths and marriages in post-war England.

Doctor, The 1992 (on video Winter 92)

★ ★ ★

Surgeon, *William Hurt*, reviews attitude to medical profession when he finds himself on other end of scalpel.

Doctor Zhivago 1965

★ ★ ★ ★

David Lean's lush treatment of *Julie Christie* and *Omar Shariffs'* ill-starred romance during Russian Revolution.

Dogfight 1991

★

River Phoenix and *Lili Taylor* lead nostalgic romantic drama with a 'looks aren't everything' message.

Do the Right Thing 1989

★ ★

Spike Leigh confronts racial issues in this part-comic, part-dramatic slice of life.

Double Crossed 1991

★

Dennis Hopper lends weight to story of a drug-smuggler who turns informant.

Dresser, The 1983

★ ★ ★

Touching tale of actor, *Albert Finney*, his assistant, *Tom Courtenay*, and their mutual reliance on one another.

Driving Miss Daisy 1989

Pleasant, beautifully-played examination of unlikely friendship between testy old southern belle, *Jessica Tandy*, and her black chauffeur, *Morgan Freeman*.

Drugstore Cowboy 1989

Matt Dillon gives fine performance in generally depressing drama of drugs and destruction.

Dry White Season, A 1989

S. African apartheid forms axis on which this absorbing tale rotates. Cameo from *Marlon Brando* adds depth.

East of Eden 1955

Steinbeck's powerful story of two brothers' rivalry for father's love. *James Dean*, in debut, exploded onto screen as the prodigal son.

Easy Rider 1969

Great, even mould-breaking in its time, but now rather dated 60's road movie featuring *Peter Fonda*, *Jack Nicholson* and *Dennis Hopper*.

Edward II 1991

Derek Jarman's absorbing, idiosyncratic version of Marlowe's play about the homosexual king.

Edward Scissorhands 1990

Johnny Depp stars as man-made boy with blades for hands exposed to 1950's smalltown America. Lovely fantasy marred by ending.

Eight Men Out 1988

Charlie Sheen and *John Cusack* in absorbing story of Chicago White Sox baseball team who threw the World Series in 1919.

84 Charing Cross Rd 1987 ★ ★ ★

Anne Bancroft and *Anthony Hopkins* charm as a book buyer and book seller corresponding across the Atlantic.

Electric Horseman, The 1979 ★ ★

Ex-rodeo star, *Robert Redford*, steals thoroughbred horse to save them both from the rat race. Journalist *Jane Fonda* investigates.

Elephant Man, The 1980

David Lynch's sentimentalized version of the life of disfigured John Merrick expertly played by *John Hurt*.

Emmanuelle 1974

Best of soft-porn movies. *Sylvia Kristel* as diplomat's wife lured into sexual deviance. At least the people look pretty.

Empire of the Sun 1987

Glossy but overlong Spielberg adaptation of J.G. Ballard's boy-hood in Japanese P.O.W. WWII camp.

Enemy of the People, An 1977

Sincere but misguided attempt by bearded *Steve McQueen* to bring Ibsen classic to screen.

Englishman Abroad, An 1985

Utterly delightful account of how actress *Carol Browne* (playing herself) met spy/traitor Guy Burgess (*Alan Bates*) in Moscow.

Entertainer, The 1960

Laurence Olivier superb as shabby, third-rate music hall star in fine adaptation of John Osborne play.

Excalibur 1981

John Boorman's lavish, quirky rendition of King Arthur fable.

Fabulous Baker Boys, The 1989

Cabaret entertainers, brothers *Beau and Jeff Bridges*, find hidden emotions exposed by the arrival of sultry singer, *Michelle Pfeiffer*.

Falcon and the Snowman, The 1985

Well-made true story of two wealthy Americans, *Sean Penn* and *Timothy Hutton*, who sold state secrets to the Russians.

Fallen Idol, The 1948

Young boy worships servant suspected of murdering wife in skilful adaptation of Grahame Greene story.

Family Business 1986   ★

Despite cast - *Sean Connery, Dustin Hoffman* and *Matthew Broderick* - this comic thriller of three generations of burglars falls flat.

Far from the Madding Crowd 1967   ★ ★ ★

Beautiful photography by Nicholas Roeg; skilful direction by John Schlesinger; sharp acting from *Julie Christie* and *Alan Bates*, in under-rated version of Hardy novel.

Field, The 1990   ★ ★

Irishman, *Richard Harris*, obsessed with a piece of land heads for tragedy in florid drama.

Fires Within, The 1963   ★ ★ ★

Louis Malle's evocative portrayal of the last 24 hours in the life of a suicide.

First of the Few, The 1942   ★ ★ ★ ★

Impressive biopic depicting life of R. J. Mitchell and events surrounding his invention of the Spitfire.

Fisher King, The 1991 (on video Summer 92)   ★ ★ ★ ★

Heartwarming 'bit of everything' story sees disillusioned D.J., *Jeff Bridges*, shown value of life by down-and-out, *Robin Williams*.

Flatliners 1990   ★ ★

Five medical students experiment with the after life. Despite cast (including *Keifer Sutherland, Kevin Bacon* and *Julia Roberts*), both dark and comic moments fall flat.

Fool, The 1991   ★ ★ ★

Lavish Victorian drama starring *Derek Jacobi* as a clerk with amazing double life. First rate British cast.

For Queen and Country 1988   ★ ★ ★

Outstanding portrayal by *Denzel Washington* of black soldier's mistreatment following demobilization from British army.

For the Boys 1991 (on video Summer 92)   ★ ★

Bette Midler and *James Caan* as couple of musicians entertaining U.S. troops through three wars. Overblown and disappointing.

Four Seasons, The 1981

Great characterization marks *Alan Alda's* poignant tale of the friendship between three couples.

Frances 1982

Outstanding portrayal by *Jessica Lange* of the tragic 1930's actress, Frances Farmer.

French Lieutenant's Woman, The 1981

 DRA

Thoughtful version of John Fowles' period novel set in modern day with *Jeremy Irons* and *Meryl Streep*, C20th lovers playing the parts of C18th soldier and the object of his desire.

From Here to Eternity 1953

Pre-WWII American military drama. Excellent performances from *Burt Lancaster*, *Deborah Kerr* and *Frank Sinatra*. Best remembered for sizzling sex scene on beach.

Front, The 1976

McCarthy witch hunt forms premise for this witty drama. *Woody Allen* as frontman for banned scriptwriters.

Gandhi 1982

Epic, Oscar-winning spectacular from Richard Attenborough about the life and death of Indian leader.

Ghost 1990

Hugely popular comedy/drama sees murdered *Patrick Swayze* returning to protect his threatened lover, *Demi Moore. Whoopi Goldberg* as medium lifts tone delightfully.

Giant 1956

Long but stylish family saga about rise of Texas oil barons, starring *Elizabeth Taylor*, *James Dean* and *Rock Hudson*.

Gilda 1946

Dramatic film noir with *Rita Hayworth* at her sexiest as the singer arousing ambivalent feelings in tough gambler, *Glen Ford*.

Gone With the Wind 1939

The classic, all-encompassing saga of the American civil war. *Vivien Leigh* and *Clark Gable* lead a host of famous names.

Goodbye Mr. Chips 1939   ★ ★ ★ ★

Robert Donat's magnificent portrayal of retiring school master who has devoted his life to his boys.

Good Morning Vietnam 1987   ★ ★ ★

Fine performance by *Robin Williams* as irreverent D.J. cheering the troops in Vietnam.

Gorillas in the Mist 1988   ★ ★ ★

Biopic about Diane Fossey, who was murdered for trying to save gorillas. Sensitively played by *Sigourney Weaver*.

Graduate, The 1967   ★ ★ ★ ★

Dustin Hoffman in unforgettable account of graduate's journey to adulthood (and adultery) via an affair with girlfriend's mother, *Anne Bancroft*.

Grand Canyon 1992 (on video Autumn 92)   ★ ★ ★

Steve Martin, Kevin Kline and *Danny Glover* lead well-written social drama about problems of living in modern, violent L.A..

Grand Hotel 1932   ★ ★ ★ ★

Berlin hotel provides backdrop for excellent character study of guests, *Greta Garbo, Joan Crawford, John and Lionel Barrymore*. Often copied but the format works best here.

Grapes of Wrath, The 1940   ★ ★ ★ ★

Compelling Steinbeck tale of workers' migration to California during the Depression. Beautifully acted by *Henry Fonda*.

Great Expectations 1946   ★ ★ ★ ★ ★

David Lean pays admirable homage to Dickens' classic story. *John Mills* as Pip, *Alec Guinness* as Herbert Pocket.

Grifters, The 1990   ★ ★ ★

Dark story of a thieving mother, *Angelica Huston*, and con-man son, *John Cusack*, never quite finds its feet.

Guess Who's Coming to Dinner? 1967   ★ ★ ★ ★

Spencer Tracy and *Katherine Hepburn* forced to come to terms with inter-racial marriage of daughter *Katharine Houghton* to *Sidney Poitier*. Tracy's last film.

Guilty by Suspicion 1991   ★ ★ ★

Rather heavy-handed account of the Hollywood victims of the 1950's Un-American Activities Committee. _Robert De Niro_ as chief suspect.

Hamlet 1948   ★ ★ ★ ★

Masterful performance and direction by _Laurence Olivier_ in the title role.

Hamlet 1991   ★ ★ ★ ★   **DRA**

Franco Zeffirelli's lucid, highly accessible version of Shakespeare's tragedy. _Mel Gibson_ excels as the prince.

Handful of Dust, A 1988   ★ ★ ★

Harrowing story from Evelyn Waugh about aristocrats seeking fulfilment. Pretty to look at, disturbing to watch.

Hangin' with the Homeboys 1991   ★ ★

Odd adventures of mixed ethnic trio on a big night out in Manhattan.

Hannah and Her Sisters 1986   ★ ★ ★ ★

Woody Allen's best plot to date concentrates on the fortunes of three sisters, _Mia Farrow_, _Barbara Hershey_ and _Dianne Wiest_.

Havana 1990   ★

Cuban politics form basis of drab 'Casablanca' rip-off. _Robert Redford_, _Raul Julia_ and _Alan Arkin_ all deserve better.

Hear My Song 1991 (on video Winter 92)   ★ ★ ★ ★

Delightful, heart-warming tale of nightclub owner trying to find noted, tax-dodging Irish tenor _Josef Locke_.

Heartbreak Kid, The 1972   ★ ★ ★

Charles Grodin tires of wife on honeymoon where he falls for _Cybil Shepherd_ in poignant, bitter-sweet Neil Simon comedy of embarrassment.

Heartburn 1986   ★ ★

Formidable cast, _Meryl Streep_ and _Jack Nicholson_, cope with marital problems but result disappoints.

Heat and Dust 1983

Merchant/Ivory story of two women, *Greta Scacchi* and *Julie Christie*, from two eras immersed in mystery and romance of India.

Henry and June 1990

Earnest and strangely dull version of Henry Miller's lusty relationship with Anais Nin.

Henry V 1944

Laurence Olivier's stirring, colourful pageant ideally suited to its time and the nation's celebration of coming victory.

Henry V 1989

Kenneth Branagh's superb, gritty contrast to Olivier's version. Olivier's troops were the Guards; Branagh's are the SAS.

Hidden Agenda 1990

Palm-sweating thriller focusing upon the British Government's dirty tricks in Northern Ireland.

Hobson's Choice 1954

Stirring yet comic performance from *Charles Laughton* as a conservative father opposed to his daughter's wedding. David Lean directed.

Homer and Eddie 1990

Hotch-potch plot about a hobo, *Whoopi Goldberg*, selfishly offering help to half-wit *James Belushi*.

Homicide 1991

Jewish cop, *Joe Mantegna*, finds his loyalties divided when he investigates sinister murder of Jewish pawn shop owner.

Hope and Glory 1987

John Boorman's delightful, nostalgic, autobiographical story of life as a small boy in England during WWII.

Howard's End 1992 (on video Winter 92)

Anthony Hopkins and *Emma Thompson* lead in well-played, good-looking adaptation of E.M. Forster's novel.

Hunchback of Notre Dame, The 1939 ★★★

The portrayal of the bell-ringing cripple by *Charles Laughton* is a tour-de-force. Remarkably touching.

Hustler, The 1961 ★★★★

Young pool shark, *Paul Newman*, stakes all to make the big-time in tensely watchable story.

If.... 1969 ★★★

Savage - if dated - satire on the British school and class system. Surreal violence originally earned it 'X' certificate.

Indian Runner 1991 (on video Summer 92) ★★

Sean Penn's glum, but not unimpressive directorial debut about two brothers on opposite sides of the law.

Inherit the Wind 1988 ★★★★

Scathing examination of 1925 prosecution of American teacher propounding Darwinian theories. *Spencer Tracy* immaculate as defense attorney.

Inn of the Sixth Happiness, The 1958 ★★★★

Touching biography of missionary Gladys Aylwood (*Ingrid Bergman*) and her trek through war-torn China with refugee children.

Intermezzo 1936 ★★

Ingrid Bergman's Hollywood debut. Weepy, moving love story with *Leslie Howard*.

In Which We Serve 1942 ★★★

Noel Coward's WWII drama about survivors of torpedoed destroyer. Dated but still splendid. *Richard Attenborough* makes his debut.

Ironweed 1987 ★

Depression-based (and depressing) drama about a couple of alcoholic down-and-outs, *Meryl Streep* and *Jack Nicholson*.

It's a Wonderful Life 1946 ★★★★★

Another Capra classic. *James Stewart* as would-be suicide shown by guardian angel what life would be like without him.

I Was Monty's Double 1958   ★ ★

True WWII story of actor, *Clifton James*, recruited to impersonate Field Marshall Montgomery in bid to fool Nazis.

Jacknife 1989   ★ ★ ★

Post-Vietnam war trauma confronted in well-acted drama. *Robert De Niro, Kathy Baker* and *Ed Harris*.

Jane Eyre 1944   ★ ★ ★

Joan Fontaine plays Charlotte Bronte's orphan heroine who falls for the enigmatic Mr. Rochester (*Orson Welles*).

Joe Versus the Volcano 1990   ★ ★

Lightweight fantasy about hypochondriac, *Tom Hanks*, conned into making himself human sacrifice. *Meg Ryan* provides romantic interest in three roles.

J. F. K. 1992   ★ ★ ★ ★

Oliver Stone's flawed but fascinating conspiracy theory about who killed J.F.K.. *Kevin Costner* leads investigation.

Julia 1977   ★ ★

Fine acting by *Jane Fonda* as Lillian Hellman, *Vanessa Redgrave* as Julia, distinguishes story of woman's ill-fated involvement with European resistance.

Julius Caesar 1953   ★ ★ ★

Fine adaptation and great cast, notably *Marlon Brando* as Mark Anthony, in spectacular version of Shakespeare's play.

Jungle Fever 1991   ★ ★ ★

Spike Leigh's sharp, angry look at black/white relationships and bigotry on both sides.

Killing Fields, The 1984   ★ ★ ★ ★

Roland Joffe's sensitive account of a reporter's harrowing experience during Cambodian war packs a hefty punch.

Killing of Sister George, The 1968   ★ ★ ★

Comic drama when an ageing lesbian, *Beryl Reid*, finds life and love crumbling around her.

Kiss of the Spider Woman 1985 ★ ★ ★

Thoughtful, sensitive tale about understanding. *William Hurt* plays the gay, Raul Julia the political activist sharing prison cell.

Kramer versus Kramer 1979 ★ ★ ★ ★

Warm-hearted drama of divorced couple, *Meryl Streep* and *Dustin Hoffman*, fighting for custody of son.

Krays, The 1990 ★ ★ ★

Hard-hitting portrait of the psychotic Cockney brothers who ruled London's East End underworld.

Last Detail, The 1973 ★ ★

Navy veterans, *Jack Nicholson* and *Otis Young*, escort kleptomaniac recruit, *Dennis Quaid*, to brig in salty, comedy/drama.

Last Emperor, The 1987 ★ ★ ★

Bernado Bertolucci's Oscar-winning dramatization of the life of Chinese Emperor Puyi.

Last Exit to Brooklyn 1989 ★

Vaguely repellent adaptation of notorious slice-of-life novel set in Brooklyn's seedier, more violent streets.

Last Tango in Paris 1973 ★ ★ ★

Butter never tasted the same after Bertolucci's erotic, explicit drama starring *Marlon Brando* and *Maria Schneider*. Infamous in its time.

Last Temptation of Christ, The 1988 ★ ★ ★

Martin Scorsese's controversial, thought-provoking drama about Jesus's self doubts. Disturbing but definitely not blasphemous.

Lean On Me 1989 ★ ★ ★

Impressive, based-on-fact school drama with *Morgan Freeman* as controversial headmaster of supposed no-hoper pupils.

Let Him Have It 1991 ★ ★ ★

Disturbing account of the Chris Craig, Derek Bentley murder trial and the latter's subsequent scandalous execution.

Letter to Three Wives, A 1949   ★ ★ ★ ★

Rich portrayal of three women's reactions to a letter from town tramp who's run off with one of their husbands.

Lion in Winter, The 1968   ★ ★ ★ ★

Atmospheric account of power struggle between Henry II (*Peter O'Toole*) and his queen, Eleanor (*Katherine Hepburn*). Splendid performances.

Little Dorrit 1988   ★ ★ ★ ★

Superb six-hour production of Dickens' social drama with *Alec Guinness* as the Marshalsea prison inmate. Great cast.

Little Man Tate 1991 (on video Summer 92)   ★ ★ ★

Jodie Foster directs and stars as inadequate mother of an eight-year-old genius pulled between her and teacher *Dianne Wiest*.

Little Women 1933   ★ ★ ★

George Cukor's version of Louisa M. Alcott's tale of family life, centring on the fortunes of the four daughters. Remade in 1949 and for TV in 1978.

Loneliness of the Long Distance Runner, The 1962   ★ ★ ★ ★

Tom Courtney first-rate as young rebel selected to represent reform school in race. *Michael Redgrave* co-stars.

Lonely Passion of Judith Hearne, The 1987   ★ ★

Lonely Irish spinster, *Maggie Smith*, finds repressed feelings stirred by charming American, *Bob Hoskins*.

Long and the Short and the Tall, The 1961   ★ ★ ★

Vivid war drama of British patrol in Malayan jungle.

Longtime Companion 1990   ★ ★ ★

Tactful handling of the effect of A.I.D.S. on homosexual community in New York.

Look Back in Anger 1958   ★ ★ ★

Richard Burton stars in screen version of John Osborne play that changed British theatre in the 1950's.

Lord of the Flies 1990   ★ ★

Aimed-at-America remake of Peter Brooks' 1963 version of Golding's novel. Solid but pedestrian.

Lost Horizon 1937   ★ ★ ★ ★

Air-crash survivor, *Ronald Colman*, discovers strange Tibetan land of love, peace and longevity in haunting Frank Capra drama.

Love Story 1970   ★ ★

Sickly sweet tale about young lovers, *Ali MacGraw* and *Ryan O'Neal*, heading for tragedy.

Macbeth 1971   ★ ★

Roman Polanski directs this violent but gripping adaptation of Shakespeare's regal play, with *Jon Finch* and *Francesca Annis*.

Magic Box, The 1951   ★ ★ ★

Every noted British actor crops up in this fascinating biopic of William Friese-Greene, one of the inventors of the movies.

Man for All Seasons, A 1966   ★ ★ ★ ★

Absorbing account of Sir Thomas Moore's fateful refusal to betray the church for his King, Henry VIII.

Man in the Moon 1991 (on video Summer 92)   ★ ★

Two young girls experience love and tragedy as they come of age in southern U.S.A.

Mask 1985   ★ ★ ★

Eric Stoltz as the young lad disfigured by lionitis and *Cher*, his mother, determined to give him a normal life. Moving story based on fact.

Matewan 1987   ★ ★ ★

John Sayles' thoughtful drama centring on rebellion of the blacks imported to break W. Virginian miners' strike in 1920.

McVicar 1980   ★ ★

Roger Daltrey rather good as convicted murderer escaping from jail. Based on McVicar's own book.

Mean Streets 1973

Martin Scorcese's riveting study of young hoods in Little Italy. With *Robert De Niro* and *Harvey Keitel*.

Medicine Man 1992 (on video Winter 92)

Sean Connery graces ecological tale of doctor seeking cancer cure in the rain forest.

Meeting Venus 1991

Glenn Close as diva of troubled opera company falling for maestro. Enjoyable example of European co-production.

Memphis 1991

Sybil Shepherd as member of kidnap gang who begins to feel sorry for their hostage.

Memphis Belle 1990

Spectacular dramatization of the 25th and final mission of B52 bomber crew during WWII. Young male talent form crew.

Men Don't Leave 1990

Penniless widow, *Jessica Lange*, struggles to bring up two young sons alone.

Metropolitan 1990

Sharply original comedy that neatly satirizes the world of young, uppercrust New York yuppies.

Midnight Express 1978

Harrowing version of Billy Hayes' experiences in Turkish jail. Phenomenally powerful direction by Alan Parker.

Millers Crossing 1990

Complex gangster movie of two Irish American hoods, *Albert Finney* and *Gabriel Byrne*, at loggerheads over woman.

Misfits, The 1961

Marilyn Monroe and *Clark Gable* as lonely, mismatched couple drawn to each other during mustang hunt in Nevada desert. Gable's last film.

Missing 1982   ★ ★ ★ ★

Excellent political thriller about a father, *Jack Lemmon*, trying to uncover mystery surrounding his son's disappearance in Chile.

Mission, The 1983   ★ ★ ★

Visually impressive but overly complex drama about a Jesuit mission to the heart of S. America.

Mississippi Burning 1988   ★ ★ ★ ★

Alan Parker's controversial but powerful account of the disappearance of three 1960's civil rights workers in deep south U.S.A..

Mississippi Masala 1991   ★ ★ ★

Denzel Washington in story of love and bigotry between American blacks and expatriate Uganda Asians.

Moderns, The 1988   ★ ★

Keith Carradine as art forger in beautiful but bland look at the 1920's arty set in Paris

Molly Maguires, The 1970   ★ ★ ★

Informer *Richard Harris* infiltrates secret 1870's group of Pennsylvania miners, headed by *Sean Connery*, who use terrorism to seek better conditions.

Month in the Country, A 1987   ★ ★ ★

Post-WWI drama about two scarred soldiers, *Colin Firth* and *Kenneth Branagh*, recovering from wartime horrors in Yorkshire village.

Mountains of the Moon 1990   ★ ★

Rival Victorian explorers, *Patrick Bergin* and *Iain Glen*, vie with each other to trace the source of the Nile.

Mrs. Miniver 1942   ★ ★ ★ ★

Greer Garson tries to keep body, soul and family together in face of encroaching WWII. Marvellous propaganda movie to encourage U.S. involvement in war.

Mr. Smith Goes to Washington 1939   ★ ★ ★ ★

Innocent school-teacher, *James Stewart*, finds nothing but corruption in U.S. Senate and bravely fights to expose it.

Murder in Mississippi 1990   ★ ★ ★

Alternative account of three civil rights workers murdered in 1964. Factually more accurate than 'Mississippi Burning'.

My Beautiful Laundrette 1985   ★ ★

Sensitive examination of racism in London's East End, experienced by Pakistani and his gay white lover.

My Girl 1991 (on video Autumn 92)   ★

Sentimental rites-of-passage stuff with *Dan Aykroyd, Macaulay Culkin* and a woefully wasted *Jamie Lee Curtis.*

My Left Foot 1989   ★ ★ ★ ★

Uplifting account of the life of Christy Brown (*Daniel Day-Lewis*) who, despite crippling cerebral palsy, became a celebrated writer.

Mystic Pizza 1988   ★ ★ ★

Sweetly appealing study of hopes, dreams and amorous adventures of three young girls; *Julia Roberts'* first movie.

Natural, The 1984   ★ ★

Curious but watchable period piece with *Robert Redford* as exceptionally - perhaps supernaturally - gifted baseball player.

Network 1976   ★ ★ ★ ★

Sidney Lumet's effective satire of the TV world. *Peter Finch* won posthumous Oscar in starring role.

New York Stories 1989   ★ ★ ★

A trilogy of short films from Woody Allen (fine), Martin Scorcese (very good), and Francis Coppolla (forget it).

Nicholas and Alexander 1971   ★ ★

Overblown epic depicting events leading to Russian Revolution and its effect on Csar Nicholas (*Michael Jayston*) and family.

9 1/2 Weeks 1986   ★

Explicit sexual activity between *Mickey Rourke* and *Kim Basinger,* but tedious story takes edge off erotica.

Norma Rae 1979   ★ ★ ★

Oscar-winning performance by *Sally Field* as a southern mill worker mobilizing a union.

Not Without My Daughter 1991   ★ ★

Sentimental, true story of American mother, *Sally Field*, attempting to recover daughter kidnapped by Iranian father, *Alfred Molina*.

Now, Voyager 1942   ★ ★ ★

Gloriously weepy melodrama with spinster, *Bette Davis*, embarked on anguished affair with married man, *Paul Heinreid*.

Officer and a Gentleman, An 1982   ★ ★ ★

Corny but well-acted story of love affair between officer-cadet, *Richard Gere*, and factory girl, *Debra Winger*.

Old Gringo 1989   ★ ★

1910 Mexican revolution the setting for spinster, *Jane Fonda*, and her adventures with journalist, *Gregory Peck*, and revolutionary, *Jimmy Smits*.

Oliver Twist 1948   ★ ★ ★ ★

Alec Guinness brilliant as Fagin in matchless David Lean version.

One Flew Over the Cuckoo's Nest 1975   ★ ★ ★ ★

Multi-Oscar winner by Milos Forman celebrates triumph of individual over the system. *Jack Nicholson* excellent.

One Good Cop 1991   ★

Incongruous mix of sentimentality and violence. Cop, *Michael Keaton*, copes with dead partner's killers and children.

On Golden Pond 1981   ★ ★ ★

Sentimental tale of family reconciliation made more poignant by featuring the estranged *Jane* and *Henry Fonda*, in his last film.

On the Waterfront 1954   ★ ★ ★ ★

Corruption amongst dock workers inspires ex-boxer, *Marlon Brando*, to fight against oppression.

Ordinary People 1980   ★ ★ ★

Robert Redford directs poignant tale of the effect of boy's suicide on family; with *Donald Sutherland* and *Mary Tyler Moore*.

Outcast of the Islands, An 1951   ★ ★ ★

Study of moral decay. *Ralph Richardson* and *Trevor Howard* as hunter and hunted on Malayan island.

Out of Africa 1985   ★ ★ ★

Great cast, *Robert Redford* and *Meryl Streep*; great scenery; mildly disappointing love story.

Panic in Needle Park, The 1971   ★ ★

Worthy film about drug abuse. *Kitty Winn* falls for and emulates heroin addict, *Al Pacino*.

Paris, Texas 1984   ★

Wim Wenders' much-praised but ultimately unsatisfying Texan road movie. *Harry Dean Stanton* and *Nastassia Kinski*.

Passage to India, A 1984   ★ ★ ★

David Lean's sumptuous adaptation of E.M. Forster's drama of east/west culture clash in 1920's.

Patton 1970   ★ ★ ★

George C. Scott superb in biopic of feisty, eccentric U.S. general in WWII.

Pickwick Papers, The 1952   ★ ★ ★

Pleasant, workmanlike version of Dickens' classic. With *James Hayter*.

Picnic at Hanging Rock 1975   ★ ★ ★

Gripping account of events leading to eerie disappearance of school-girls and their teacher during school outing.

Place in the Sun, A 1951   ★ ★

Overblown tragedy of social-climber, *Montgomery Clift*, sacrificing love of working girl for wealthy *Elizabeth Taylor*.

Places in the Heart 1984   ★ ★

Plucky *Sally Field* as farmer's widow struggling during Depression to keep her Texas farm.

Pope of Greenwich Village, The 1984   ★ ★ ★

Sharply observed study of New York hustler, *Mickey Rourke*, reluctantly involved with cousin, *Eric Roberts*, in mad schemes.

Pork Chop Hill 1959   ★ ★ ★

Gregory Peck defending vital hill against on-coming Korean army in rugged war story.

Pretty Woman 1990   ★ ★ ★ ★ ★

Irresistable fairytale of hooker, *Julia Roberts*, falling in love with wealthy businessman client, *Richard Gere*.

Prick up your Ears 1987   ★ ★ ★

Gary Oldman very impressive as British playwright Joe Orton; *Alfred Molina* plays his lover who ultimately kills him.

Pride and Prejudice 1940   ★ ★ ★ ★

Pleasing, though hardly faithful, version of Jane Austen's delightful romance stars *Greer Garson* and *Laurence Olivier*.

Prime of Miss Jean Brodie, The 1969   ★ ★ ★ ★

Maggie Smith as avant-garde schoolmistress steering her charges towards womanhood is both funny and touching.

Prince of the City, The 1981   ★ ★ ★

Treat Williams as cop who exposes corruption within N.Y. police force and becomes villain rather than hero. Based on true story.

Prince of Tides, The 1992 (on video Summer 92)   ★ ★ ★ ★

Barbara Streisand's melodramatic love story. *Nick Nolte* the man with a disturbed past; Streisand the psychiatrist making him confront it.

Private Lives of Elizabeth and Essex, The 1939   ★ ★

Bette Davis the Queen, *Errol Flynn* the dashing Lord Essex for whom she's prepared to sacrifice everything - well, almost.

Proof 1991

Distrustful blind man uses photography to ensure people tell him the truth in absorbing Australian story.

Prospero's Books 1991

Myriad of impressive visuals but style better than content in Peter Greenaway's version of 'The Tempest'.

Pumping Iron 1977

Documentary about body builders with young _Arnold Schwarzenegger_ going for Mr. Olympia title.

Pump Up the Volume 1990

Teenage movie with _Christian Slater_ a high school kid by day, a pirate radio D.J. by night.

Punchline 1988

Oddly glum tale about comedy. Stand-up comic, _Tom Hanks_, teaches housewife, _Sally Field_, how to make people laugh.

Quare Fellow, The 1962

Irish drama of prison guard, _Patrick McGoohan_, forced to revise his views on capital punishment.

Queen Christina 1933

Probably _Garbo's_ best dramatic role as Swedish queen relinquishing throne for love.

Quiet Man, The 1952

Sentimental, romanticized vehicle for _John Wayne_ as ex-boxer settling in Irish village full of usual boozy stereotypes.

Raging Bull 1980

Martin Scorsese's study of boxing champion Jake La Motta (_Robert De Niro_). Perhaps the best film of its kind in the 1980's.

Ragtime 1981

Socially aware drama of racism in turn-of-century America. Notable for inducing _James Cagney_ out of twenty-year retirement.

Rain Man 1988   ★ ★ ★ ★

Relationship of autistic savant, *Dustin Hoffman*, and initially ruthless brother, *Tom Cruise*. Two fine performances.

Rambling Rose 1991   ★ ★ ★

1930's family life disrupted by arrival of promiscuous child of nature, *Laura Dern*, in home of *Robert Duvall* and *Diane Ladd*.

Reach for the Sky 1956   ★ ★ ★   **DRA**

Solid account of exploits of WWII flying ace Douglas Bader (*Kenneth Moore*) despite double leg amputation.

Rebecca 1940   ★ ★ ★ ★

Daphne Du Maurier's romantic saga of young bride haunted by memory of husband's first wife. With *Joan Fontaine* and *Laurence Olivier*.

Rebel Without a Cause 1955   ★ ★ ★

James Dean's angry young man looks dated now but still bears emotional resonance of teenage alienation.

Red Badge of Courage, The 1951   ★ ★ ★ ★

John Huston's civil war story with *Audie Murphy* as young soldier guilt-stricken over his cowardice.

Reds 1981   ★ ★ ★

Warren Beatty's Oscar-winning directorial debut about American journalist's espousal of communism. *Beatty* and *Diane Keaton* star.

Red Shoes, The 1948   ★ ★ ★ ★ ★

Marvellous, innovative tale about the staging of a ballet and a young dancer, *Moira Shearer*, torn between two men.

Regarding Henry 1991   ★ ★

Harrison Ford as ruthless lawyer whose attitude to family and work changes drastically after he's shot.

Repulsion 1965   ★ ★ ★

Roman Polanski's psychological shocker depicts mental deterioration of depressed *Catherine Deneuve*, left alone in London.

Reversal of Fortune 1990

Impeccable performance by *Jeremy Irons* as Claus Von Bulow, accused of trying to murder his wealthy wife, *Glenn Close*.

Richard III 1955

Laurence Olivier's performance as Crookback scared generations of actors away from the role. Good, if stagey, production.

River, The 1951

Jean Renoir's poetic study of British children growing up in Bengal.

Rocking Horse Winner, The 1950

Unusual, moving D.H. Lawrence story of small boy with knack of picking racetrack winners.

Roger & Me 1989

Michael Moore's extraordinary documentary exposes the despair of a Michigan town when General Motors moved out.

Roman Holiday 1953

Touching, tender romance between runaway princess, *Audrey Hepburn*, and journalist, *Gregory Peck*.

Room with a View, A 1985

Beautiful adaptation of E.M. Foster's Italian-based tale of English manners. Photography and British cast superb.

Rumble Fish 1983

Intense, over-stylized drama of teenager, *Matt Dillon*, manipulated by older brother, *Mickey Rourke*.

Rush 1992 (on video Autumn 92)

Hard-hitting drama of narcotics cops, *Jennifer Jason Leigh* and *Jason Patric*, working under cover and becoming addicts themselves.

Russia House, The 1990

Sean Connery as London publisher embroiled in wordy, post cold war Russian espionage. *Michelle Pfeiffer*, the Moscow love interest.

DRA

Ryan's Daughter 1970   ★ ★ ★

David Lean's overblown - but underrated - story of young wife, *Sara Miles*, and her love affair with shell-shocked British soldier in small Irish community.

Salvador 1986

Oliver Stone's powerful, sobering account of experiences of journalist Richard Boyle (*James Wood*) in war-torn El Salvador.

Same Time Next Year 1978

Sweet story of a couple, *Ellen Burstyn* and *Alan Alda* who meet for a brief adulterous affair every year. Low-key but charming.

Saturday Night and Sunday Morning 1960   ★ ★ ★

Albert Finney plays angry young man whose pride becomes belligerence.

Scandal 1989   ★ ★ ★

Absorbing examination of the Profumo Affair which eventually brought down British government in the 1960's. Lovely performances by *John Hurt, Joanne Whalley-Kilmer* and *Bridget Fonda*.

Secret Honor 1984

Philip Baker Hall excels in this astonishing one man show directed by Robert Altman and based on the alleged ravings of a suicidal Richard Nixon. Really chilling stuff.

Servant, The 1963   ★ ★ ★

Sexual undertones create atmosphere and tension in psychological horror as *Dirk Bogard*, the cunning manservant, becomes master of his employer, *James Fox*.

Sex, Lies and Videotapes 1989

Astonishing directorial debut of Steven Soderbergh with story of small town mental and extra-marital relationships. *Peter Gallagher, James Spader, Andie Macdowell* and *Laura San Giacomo* all superb.

Shadowlands 1985

Joss Ackland as C.S.Lewis in this touching, rewarding account of writer's love affair with American divorcee, *Claire Bloom*.

Shampoo 1975   ★ ★ ★

Hip, sexy and very 70's satire of Californian morals. *Warren Beatty* as the hairdresser servicing his demanding clientele, *Julie Christie* and *Goldie Hawn* amongst others.

Sheltering Sky, The 1990

Drab, period reconstruction of Paul Bowle's famous novel about a couple, *John Malkovich* and *Debra Winger*, discovering North Africa after WWII.

Shooting Party, The 1984

Deeply moving examination of class and culture centring on a weekend shooting party in 1913. *James Mason* quite brilliant in his last role.

Silkwood 1983

Powerful rendition of Karen Silkwood story. *Meryl Streep* as the woman who uncovered secret at nuclear plant. *Cher*, her best friend and colleague.

Six Wives of Henry VIII, The 1972

Scintillating TV drama casts *Keith Michell*, excellent as the ambitious young king growing into a disillusioned, tyrannical monarch.

Sophie's Choice 1982

Meryl Streep's heartrending performance as the survivor of Nazi concentration camp struggling to find happiness in America.

Sound Barrier, The 1952

Soaring cinematography; solid performances by *Ralph Richardson* and *Ann Todd*, plus David Lean's direction distinguish this tale of the courageous men who tested the early jet planes.

Spymaker; The Secret Life of Ian Fleming 1990

Fictionalized biography of 'James Bond' creator. Nice touch casting Sean's son, *Jason Connery*, in title role.

Stand and Deliver 1987

Gentle, based-on-fact, drama of Hispanic headmaster adopting unorthodox methods to ensure his drug-pushing, gang-member pupils win qualifications.

Stand by Me 1986

Affectionate, nostalgic glimpse of boyhood friendship in 1950's America.

Stanley and Iris 1990

Poverty-stricken woman, *Jane Fonda*, finds love when teaching dyslexic, *Robert De Niro*, to read. Pretty dull.

Steel Magnolias 1989   ★ ★ ★ ★

Bittersweet comedy following the lives of female friends in small Louisiana town: *Julia Roberts, Shirley MacLaine, Sally Field, Dolly Parton, Darryl Hannah* and *Olympia Dukakis*.

Stella 1989   ★ ★

Presence of *Bette Midler*, sassy in title role, almost saves story of woman's lone fight to raise daughter in remake of Stella Dallas.

Stepping Out 1991   ★ ★ ★

Liza Minelli runs a tap-dance class of unfulfilled women and one man. All need the help and friendship the class provides. *Julie Walters* lightens tone.

Strapless 1989   ★

David Hare directed his own story of an American doctor, *Blair Brown*, who marries on a whim and regrets it. Good performances by Brown and Jane's niece, *Bridget Fonda*.

Streetcar Named Desire, A 1951   ★ ★ ★ ★

Powerful Tennesse Williams melodrama. Great performances by Oscar-winning *Vivien Leigh, Kim Hunter, Karl Malden* and especially by *Marlon Brando* who, alone, missed an Oscar. Why?

Sunset Boulevard 1950   ★ ★ ★ ★

Billy Wilder's subtly vicious indictment of Hollywood. *William Holden* as young writer tragically involved with has-been movie star, *Gloria Swanson*.

Tale of Two Cities, A 1935   ★ ★ ★

Lavish version of Dickens classic set during the French Revolution. *Ronald Colman* and *Elizabeth Allan* lead.

Talk Radio 1988   ★ ★ ★

Eric Bogosian as radio talk-show host whose controversial style wins notoriety and worse in Oliver Stone's grim moral tale.

Ten Commandments, The 1956   ★ ★ ★ ★

Cecil B. De Mille's biblical epic. Cast of thousands. *Charlton Heston* as Moses, *Yul Brynner* as Pharoah.

Tender Mercies 1983   ★ ★

Poignant performance from *Robert Duvall* as down-at-heel country singer rebuilding his life around young widow, *Tess Harper*, and her son.

10 Rillington Place 1970 ★ ★ ★

Solid account of the John Christie/Timothy Evans murder case in 1940s. *Richard Attenborough, Judy Geeson* and *John Hurt* give their all.

Terms of Endearment 1983 ★ ★

Sub-plot involving *Jack Nicholson* and *Shirley MacLaine* is funny but sentimentality of main plot where daughter, *Debra Winger*, is dying from cancer, sticks in the throat.

Texasville 1990 ★ ★

Disappointing follow-up to 'The Last Picture Show', resuming life stories of *Jeff Bridges, Cybil Shepherd, Timothy Bottoms* and *Randy Quaid* in the 1980's.

They Shoot Horses, Don't They? 1969 ★ ★ ★

Bleak view of America during the Depression in a story of marathon dancing contests which sometimes lasted for weeks. *Jane Fonda* stars.

Third Man, The 1949 ★ ★ ★ ★

Superb thriller based in post-war Austria. *Joseph Cotton* as a naive American summoned to Vienna by friend, *Orson Welles*, only to discover he's died. A movie classic.

Three Faces of Eve, The 1957 ★ ★ ★

Powerful performance by *Joanne Woodward* as a schizophrenic with three diverse lives.

Tiger Bay 1959 ★ ★

A lonely young girl, *Hayley Mills*, is abducted by a murderer on the run. Sensitive story, nicely performed. Hayley's daddy, *John Mills*, stars.

Time of Your Life, The 1948 ★ ★

Decent cast, (including *James Cagney*) in plodding tale about inhabitants of Nick's Saloon.

To Kill a Mockingbird 1962 ★ ★ ★ ★

Rich drama based in deep south U.S.A., concentrating upon family of a lawyer, *Gregory Peck*, defending negro accused of rape.

Torch Song Trilogy 1988 ★ ★ ★

Evocative and emotional comedy/drama told in three parts about a homosexual, *Harvey Fierstein*, coming to terms with his problems.

To Sir, with Love 1967 ★ ★ ★

Highly competent account of black school teacher, *Sidney Poitier*, earning respect and devotion of unruly pupils.

Town like Alice, A 1956 ★ ★ ★

Powerful story of female P.O.W.'s in Malaysia, headed by *Virginia McKenna*, helped by *Peter Finch*.

Truly, Madly, Deeply 1991 ★ ★ ★ ★

Alternately touching and hilarious tale of coming to terms with grief. *Juliet Stevenson*, the woman, trying to accept the death of her partner, *Alan Rickman*.

Twelve Angry Men 1957 ★ ★ ★ ★

Terrific court-room drama focusing on the deliberations of a murder case jury. Cast headed by *Henry Fonda*. Brilliant directorial debut by Sidney Lumet.

Ugly American, The 1963 ★ ★ ★

Far from ugly *Marlon Brando* plays Ambassador (to Communist Asian country) whose mistakes threaten political and personal disaster.

Unbearable Lightness of Being, The 1988 ★ ★ ★

Intelligent, absorbing character study, adapted from Milan Kundera's novel, of a doctor, *Daniel Day-Lewis*, reluctantly involved in political and sexual conflict.

Valmont 1989 ★ ★

Miles Forman's version of Chodelos de Laclos' story of sex, corruption and decadence in C18th France. 'Dangerous Liaisons' is better.

Verdict, The 1982 ★ ★ ★

Disillusioned, dead-beat lawyer, *Paul Newman*, gets his act together to fight case of medical negligence. Splendidly directed by Sidney Lumet.

Voyager 1992 (on video Winter 92) ★ ★ ★

Sam Shephard's absorbing personal voyage of discovery leads towards Greek tragedy.

Wall Street 1987 ★ ★ ★

Oliver Stone's bleak indictment of greed and corruption among stock brokers, *Michael Douglas* and *Charlie Sheen*.

War and Peace 1956 ★ ★

Simplified King Vidor version of Tolstoy's epic. *Audrey Hepburn, Henry Fonda* and *John Mills*. Spectacular battle scenes.

War of the Roses, The 1989 ★ ★ ★ ★

Achingly funny black comedy about marriage turning sour. *Kathleen Turner* and *Michael Douglas* as warring partners.

Watership Down 1978 ★ ★ ★

Animated feature version of Richard Adams' best-seller. A family of rabbits face danger and death as they search for a new home. A bit violent for the very young.

Welcome Home, Roxy Carmichael 1990 ★ ★ ★

Enigmatic comedy about lonely young girl, *Wynona Ryder*, adapting to adoption and relationships.

Whatever Happened to Baby Jane? 1962 ★ ★ ★ ★

Wild, over-the-top black comedy of two sisters tormenting one another. Magnificently hammy performances by a demented *Bette Davis* and a crippled *Joan Crawford*.

When the Whales Come 1989 ★ ★ ★

Deaf loner, *Paul Schofield*, and two young children try to save a beached whale from hungry islanders. Unusual, off-beat story.

Where No Vultures Fly 1951 ★ ★

British docudrama relating conception of Mount Kilimanjaro Game reserve in Africa. *Anthony Steele* and *Dinah Sheridan*.

White Hunter, Black Heart 1990 ★ ★

Clint Eastwood as a thinly-disguised John Huston:- a director more obsessed with shooting an elephant than his movie. (Incidentally, the movie was 'The African Queen'.)

White Mischief 1988 ★ ★

Lusty sex and murder saga of expatriate community in Kenya with *Greta Scacchi, Charles Dance* and *Joss Ackland*.

White Palace 1990 ★ ★ ★

Sexy drama with *James Spader*, a yuppie widower falling for older, down-trodden waitress, *Susan Sarandon*.

Who's Afraid of Virginia Woolf? 1966   ★ ★ ★ ★

Elizabeth Taylor and *Richard Burton*, a perfect partnership, as academic couple in ferocious marital relationship.

Whose Life is it Anyway? 1981   ★ ★ ★

Richard Dreyfuss magnificent as dynamic artist, paralysed in an accident, fighting for his right to die.

Winslow Boy, The 1950   ★ ★ ★ ★   DRA

Superb drama casts *Robert Donat* as barrister employed to clear name of *Cedric Hardwicke's* son, no matter the cost to self or family.

Women in Love 1970   ★ ★

Ken Russell's raunchy version of D.H. Lawrence's tale of love and sex. *Glenda Jackson, Alan Bates* and *Oliver Reed*. Famous (notorious?) nude, male wrestling scene.

Wooden Horse, The 1950   ★ ★ ★

Solid British wartime escape drama with *Leo Genn* and *David Tomlinson*.

World Apart, A 1988   ★ ★ ★

Highly charged drama set in S. Africa. *Barbara Hershey's* bitter struggle against apartheid seen through eyes of her daughter, *Johdi May*.

Yanks 1979   ★ ★ ★

Engaging story of Americans billeted in small-town England during WWII and the lives and loves they leave behind. *Richard Gere* leads.

Young Lions, The 1958   ★ ★ ★ ★

A blonde *Marlon Brando* takes some getting used to but this is a gripping WWII story told from both the German and American point of view.

Young Soul Rebels 1991   ★

Black, British drama/murder story about two D.J.s - one straight, the other gay - at a funky pirate radio station. Set in 1970's.

Zorba the Greek 1964   ★ ★ ★

Drama based in small village on Crete where colourful native, *Anthony Quinn*, teaches Englishman *Alan Bates* how to get most out of life.

Addam's Family, The 1991 (on video Summer 92)   (cert PG)   ★ ★ ★

Ghoulish comic strip family brought to life Hollywood-style by *Angelica Huston, Raul Julia* and *Christopher Lloyd*.

All Dogs Go to Heaven 1989   (cert U)   ★ ★

Disney-style animation made in Ireland. *Burt Reynolds* provides voice of the canine hero.

All I Want For Christmas 1991 (on video Autumn 92)   (cert U)   ★

Sentimental tale centring on children's scheme to reunite parents.

American Tail, An 1986   (cert U)   ★ ★ ★   **FAM**

Spielberg's animated fantasy of Russian mouse family emigrating to an America whose streets, they hope, are paved with cheese.

American Tail II: Fievel Goes West 1991 (on video Autumn 92)   (cert U)   ★ ★

The Mousekewitz's in the wild west.

Anne of Green Gables 1985   (cert U)   ★ ★

Spirited orphan, *Megan Follows*, wins love of lonely old couple.

Arachnaphobia 1990   (cert PG)   ★ ★

Slick, Spielberg produced, comic thriller about small town overrun by killer spiders.

Around the World in 80 Days 1965   (cert U)   ★ ★ ★

Phileas Fogg (*David Niven*) wagers he can tour the globe in 80 days. Glittering cast of guest stars help or hinder.

Back to the Future 1985   (cert PG)   ★ ★ ★ ★

Michael J. Fox sent to the past to ensure his future in a terrific movie. First and best of the series.

Back to the Future II 1989   (cert PG)   ★ ★

Too fast, too complex, too harsh sequel has *Fox* and nutty professor, *Christopher Lloyd*, zipping through time like yo-yos.

Back to the Future III 1990   (cert PG)

Back on form, *Fox* and *Lloyd* find themselves in the wild west where Lloyd finds romance.

Beethoven 1991 (on video Autumn 92)   (cert U)

A St. Bernard dog causes amusing chaos for canine-hater, *Charles Grodin*, and family and rounds up the bad guys.

Beetlejuice 1988   (cert 15)

Comic caper of ghosts, *Alec Baldwin* and *Geena Davis*, trying to exorcise modernist family from home with help of whacky Betelgeuse, *Michael Keaton*.

Big 1988   (cert PG)

Tom Hanks gives spirited performance as a twelve-year-old in adult body and world.

Bingo 1991 (on video Summer 92)   (cert PG)

Quirky story based around the world's smartest dog.

Born Free 1966   (cert U)

Visually stunning biopic of Joy Adamson raising orphaned lion in Kenya. *Virginia McKenna* and *Bill Travers* lead.

Bugsy Malone 1976   (cert U)

Alan Parker directs cast of children in 1920's gangster musical. Enjoyable romp. Twelve-year-old *Jodie Foster* stars.

Captain America 1979   (cert U)

Son of legendary comic strip hero fights nuclear threat posed by arch criminal.

Crocodile Dundee 1986   (cert 15)

Surprisingly but deservedly successful yarn of outback woodsman, *Paul Hogan*, uprooted to Manhattan. Great fun.

Crocodile Dundee 2 1988   (cert PG)

More violence, fewer jokes as *Paul Hogan* leaves Manhattan and returns to Oz to trap drug dealers.

Curly Sue 1991 (on video Summer 92)   (cert PG)   ★

Slushy John Hughes comedy. Precocious little girl gets a mother for Christmas.

Dark Crystal, The 1983   (cert PG)   ★ ★

Jim Henson's dark, superbly animated fable of good and evil.

Dumbo 1941   (cert U)   ★ ★ ★

Wealth of characters makes Disney's animation of a flying elephant always worth watching.

Fantasia 1940   (cert U)   ★ ★ ★ ★

Walt Disney's stunning, innovative blend of animation and classical music. A minor work of art.

Field of Dreams 1989   (cert PG)   ★ ★ ★ ★ ★

Perfectly enchanting fantasy of a farmer, *Kevin Costner*, told by a disembodied voice to build baseball pitch in middle of crops so that late, great players may return. Magical.

Flash Gordon 1980   (cert PG)   ★ ★

Comic strip hero bought to life by *Sam J. Jones*, in lavish sci-fi adventure. Good designs, score, supporting cast.

Frog Prince, The 1987   (cert U)   ★ ★ ★

Delightful modern-day fairytale set against beautiful Parisian backdrop.

Ghostbusters 1984   (cert PG)   ★ ★ ★ ★

Who you gonna call if plagued by ghosts? *Dan Akroyd*, *Harold Ramis* and *Bill Murray*. Rib-tickling comedy with scary special effects.

Ghostbusters II 1989   (cert PG)   ★ ★ ★

Old gang return with fewer laughs, more violence as they battle a New Year's Eve explosion of spirits.

Golden Voyage of Sinbad, The 1974   (cert U)   ★ ★

Colourful adaptation of Arabian Nights adventure. Special effects better than the acting.

Great Expectations 1946   (cert PG)   ★ ★ ★ ★ ★

David Lean pays admirable homage to Dickens' classic story. *John Mills* as Pip, *Alec Guinness* as Herbert Pocket.

Gremlins 1984   (cert 15)   ★ ★ ★ ★

Cute little creatures turn vicious if fed after midnight in adult children's story from the Spielberg stable.

Gremlins 2: The New Batch 1990   (cert 15)   ★ ★

Effects are an improvement on original but story's weaker.

Harvey 1950   (cert U)   ★ ★ ★ ★ ★

Sheer delight about an endearing drunk, *James Stewart*, whose relatives want him committed because his best friend is an invisible, six-foot rabbit.

Home Alone 1990   (cert PG)   ★ ★ ★

Eight-year-old *Macaulay Culkin*, mistakenly left at home alone for Christmas, fights off burglars and discovers the value of family life. Overly sentimental but amusing.

Honey, I Shrunk the Kids 1989   (cert U)   ★ ★ ★

Scientist, *Rick Moranis*, mistakenly shrinks children to microscopic size. Family fun as kids fight for survival.

It's a Wonderful Life 1946   (cert U)   ★ ★ ★ ★ ★

Another Capra classic. *James Stewart* as would-be suicide shown by guardian angel what life would be like without him.

Jason and the Argonauts 1963   (cert U)   ★ ★ ★

Harryhausen special effects dominate legendary adventure of search for the Golden Fleece.

Lady and the Tramp, The 1955   (cert U)   ★ ★ ★ ★

Timeless Disney delight. Animated adventures of well-bred spaniel and her raffish mongrel boyfriend.

Lionheart 1987   (cert PG)   ★

A band of youngsters led by *Eric Stoltz* search for missing King Richard and defend his throne.

Little Kidnappers, The 1953   (cert U)

Tidy children's tale of two orphans, living with testy grandpa in Nova Scotia, who find abandoned baby and keep it.

Little Mermaid, The 1989   (cert U)

Disney's delightful - though much softened- adaptation of Hans Christian Anderson fairytale.

Little Princess, The 1939   (cert U)

Shirley Temple at her cutest as poor little rich girl cruelly mistreated at boarding school.

Local Hero 1983   (cert PG) **FAM**

Bill Forsyth's delightful examination of effect on Scottish coastal village when American tycoon wants to buy it for oil refinery.

Love Bug, The 1969   (cert U)

Herbie's first and best outing as the VW Beetle with a mind of its own.

Mary Poppins 1964   (cert U)

Musical version of the no-nonsense, magical nanny. *Julie Andrews* badly miscast and *Dick Van Dyke* unconvincing as her cockney beau.

Meet the Applegates 1991   (cert 15)

Insects in human guise plot to end the world in weak but inoffensive fable.

Mermaids 1990   (cert 15)

Terrific little comedy featuring *Cher* as single mother unable to settle. *Winona Ryder*, *Bob Hoskins* and sound-track provide great support.

Miracle on 34th Street 1947   (cert U)

Enchanting fantasy of department store Santa put on trial to prove he really is Father Christmas. With *Maureen O'Hara* and *Edmund Gwenn*.

Moonstruck 1987   (cert PG)

Enchanting romantic comedy set in Little Italy where *Cher* falls in love with fiancée's brother, Nicholas Cage.

National Velvet 1944   (cert U)   ★ ★ ★

Well-loved family movie. *Elizabeth Taylor* determined to ride her horse to victory in the Grand National.

Never Ending Story, The 1984   (cert U)   ★ ★ ★

Children's adventure about small boy entering the magical land in his story book. Good effects.

Never Ending Story 2 1990   (cert U)   ★ ★

Plot's a little weak but effects still impress in a further adventure set in Fantasia.

Nukie 1992   (cert U)   ★

Two cute aliens separated on earth are reunited by African children.

Prancer 1989   (cert U)

Children's fable of unhappy little girl who finds Santa's missing reindeer.

Princess Bride, The 1987   (cert PG)   ★ ★ ★ ★

Enchanting fairytale adventure in which abducted princess, *Robin Wright*, must be rescued by dashing hero, *Cary Elwes*.

Prisoner of Zenda, The 1952   (cert U)   ★ ★ ★

Very acceptable re-make of classic 1937 Ronald Colman movie, this time starring *Stewart Granger*.

Railway Children, The 1972   (cert U)   ★ ★ ★ ★ ★

Three children adapt to new life in the country when father's imprisoned on spying charge. Little gem of a picture.

Rescuers, The 1977   (cert U)

Animated adventure involving exploits of trouble-shooting mice.

Rescuers Down Under, The 1990   (cert U)

International Rescue Aid dispatches the two brave mice to save Australian boy in deep trouble.

Rock a Doodle 1991   (cert U)

Animated farm-yard adventure about an Elvis lookalike Cockerel who heads for the bright lights of the city.

Short Circuit 1986   (cert PG)

A cutesy robot comes to life to the surprise of its creator, *Steve Guttenberg*. Acceptable, sci-fi comedy.

Splash 1984   (cert PG)

Humorous fairytale set in modern-day where *Tom Hanks* unknowingly falls in love with a mermaid, *Darryl Hannah*.

Star Trek: The Motion Picture 1979   (cert U)

FAM

Disappointing film version of the marvellous TV series. Starship Enterprise crew battle to save earth from threatening force field. Star Trek's II, III and V not up to much.

Star Trek IV: The Voyage Home 1986   (cert PG)

Ecological message as the Enterprise land on C20th Earth to save the whales.

Star Trek VI: The Undiscovered Country 1991 (on video Autumn 92) (cert PG)

Best and final adventure of the old guard (*Shatner et al*). Enterprise must escort implacable enemies, the Klingons, to Inter-Galactic peace conference. Chaos ensues.

Star Wars 1977   (cert U)

Marvellous classic sci-fi adventure. *Mark Hamill, Harrison Ford, Carrie Fisher, Alec Guinness* and robots (R2D2, C-3PO), in hugely imaginative Inter-Galactic western.

Superman 1978 and II 1980   (cert PG)

Much as you'd expect. *Christopher Reeve* as Superman, *Margot Kidder* as Lois Lane and such assorted villains as *Gene Hackman, Terence Stamp* and *Richard Pryor*.

Superman III 1983 and IV 1987   (cert PG) ★ ★

The mixture pretty much as before.

Talk of the Town, The 1942   (cert U) ★ ★ ★ ★ ★

Great romantic comedy. *Cary Grant* an escaped convict hiding out in *Jean Arthur's* home, rented by Supreme Court judge, *Ronald Colman*.

Teenage Mutant Ninja Turtles 1990   (cert PG)   ★ ★

Four mutated amphibians fight New York crimewave from their home in the sewers. So-so mix of action and comedy.

Teenage Mutant Ninja Turtles II 1991   (cert PG)   ★ ★

Pizza-loving dudes return to wage war on toxic waste. Young viewers should find it as pleasing - or not - as the first.

Watership Down 1978   (cert U)   ★ ★ ★

Animated feature version of Richard Adams' best-seller. A family of rabbits face danger and death as they search for a new home. A bit violent for the very young.

White Fang 1991   (cert 15)   ★ ★

Ethan Hawke prospecting for gold in Klondike finds friends; orphan wolf cub and _Klaus Maria Brandauer_.

Who Framed Roger Rabbit? 1988   (cert PG)   ★ ★ ★ ★

Outstanding animation combined with live action marks comic caper of detective, _Bob Hoskins_, out to clear the name of wrongly accused rabbit.

Willow 1988   (cert PG)   ★ ★

Fantasy adventure of a dwarf guarding a baby saviour with the help of _Val Kilmer_ and _Joanne Whalley-Kilmer_.

Witches, The 1990   (cert PG)   ★ ★ ★

At a British hotel, a small boy and his granny find themselves in the middle of a witches convention headed by _Angelica Huston_.

Wizard of Oz, The 1939   (cert U)   ★ ★ ★ ★ ★

Shirley Temple was initial choice for Dorothy but mercifully, _Judy Garland_ stepped into the ruby slippers for this enchanting fantasy musical.

Wolves of Willoughby Chase, The 1989   (cert PG)   ★

Two young children left to the wicked wiles of _Mel Smith_ and _Stephanie Beecham_.

Assault, The 1986

Thought-provoking drama of Dutch survivor of WWII tracing events that led to slaughter of his family.

Babette's Feast 1987

This delightful Danish tale about two spinsters accommodating mysterious female stranger, *Stephanie Audran*, is a gourmet's delight.

Battleship Potemkin 1925 ★★★★★

Eisenstein's great silent movie about the crew of a Russian battleship during the mutiny at Odessa.

Betty Blue 1986 ★★

Visually stunning French film of mad waitress and odd job man travelling around country. Noted for opening sex scenes.

Blue Angel, The 1930 ★★

FOR

German craftsmanship brings to life story of school-teacher obsessed with cabaret artist. The film that made *Marlene Dietrich* an international star.

Cinema Paradiso 1988

Italian gem about young boy's love of the cinema. Steeped in charm, especially the early section.

Claire's Knee 1971 ★★

One of Eric Rohmer's moral tales. Engaged young man becomes obsessed with knee of girl he doesn't even like.

Cyrano De Bergerac 1990 ★★★★★

Outstanding adaptation of Rostand play with *Gérard Depardieu* superb as the poet, swordsman and vicarious lover.

Danton 1982

Gérard Depardieu memorable in Andrzei Wajda's dramatic reconstruction of the Reign of Terror.

Delicatessen 1991 (on video Autumn 92)

Shocking, funny French tale that hovers between farce and horror centred on cannibalistic inhabitants of apartment block.

Diva 1982

Stylish high-tec melodrama about French music lover unwittingly involved with underworld after illicitly taping a diva's concert.

Everybody's Fine 1990

The darker side of nostalgia in Italian tale of old man, *Marcello Mastroianni*, on visit to family finding everybody's not as fine as he thought.

Fanny and Alexander 1983

Sumptuous family saga by Ingmar Bergman which concentrates on the fortunes of two children in turn-of-the-century Sweden.

Fitzcarraldo 1982

Klaus Kinski excels in German film about one man's attempt to bring the great Caruso to out-of-way town.

Hiroshima Mon Amour 1960

Alain Resnais' unusual, thoughtful story about love affair of French actress and Japanese architect in post-war Hiroshima.

Jean de Florette 1986

Beautifully shot, perfectly acted French country soap. *Gérard Depardieu*, the farmer, duped by conniving neighbour, *Yves Montand*.

Jesus of Montreal 1989

Denis Arcaud's morality play in which actor, *Lothaire Bluteau*, portraying Jesus is mistaken for the real thing.

Kagemusha 1980

C16th Japanese thief poses as dead warlord to safeguard throne in Kurosawa's marvellous epic.

La Balance 1982

Violent French crime story. Prostitute and petty criminal pressed to give evidence against crime boss.

La Cage Aux Folles 1978

Very funny French comedy. Two gay lovers pose as straights when son of one of them wants to get married.

La Dolce Vita 1960   ★ ★ ★ ★

Fellini's surreal Italian drama of reporter *Marcello Mastroianni's* adventures in decadent Roman society. Bit dated now.

La Regle du Jeu 1932   ★ ★ ★ ★ ★

Jean Renoir's abiding classic comedy/drama of morals and mores at pre-war French weekend party.

La Ronde 1950   ★ ★ ★

Max Ophul's delicious French farce in which chain of illicit love affairs comes full circle.

Manon des Sources 1986   ★ ★ ★ ★

Equally impressive sequel to 'Jean De Florettes'. *Gérard Depardieu's* daughter seeks revenge on *Yves Montand*.

Mephisto 1981   ★ ★ ★ ★   **FOR**

Klaus Maria Brandauer superb as actor whose ambition means selling out to the Nazis in forceful German drama.

Mon Oncle 1958   ★ ★ ★

Jacques Tati's hilarious send-up of modern, gadget-ridden society.

Monsieur Hire 1989   ★ ★ ★

Peeping Tom falls in love with beautiful neighbour involved in murder. Taut, tense adaptation of Simenon story.

Monsieur Hulot's Holiday 1953   ★ ★ ★

Jacques Tati as accident prone bachelor causing chaos at the seaside.

My Father's Glory 1991   ★ ★ ★

Marcel Pagnol's charming account of his childhood in southern France during early part of century.

My Life as a Dog 1985   ★ ★ ★ ★

Poignant Swedish comedy about mischievous boy sent to live with aunt and uncle.

My Mother's Castle 1991

Marcel Pagnol continues his reminiscences of French childhood in companion piece to 'My Father's Glory'.

Nasty Girl, The 1990 (on video Autumn 92)

Fine blend of humour and drama in young woman's attempt to uncover her hometown's guilty, Nazi past.

Padre Padrone 1977   ★ ★

Italian biopic of brutalized Sardinian peasant boy who grew up to be a scholar. Worthy but unmemorable.

Pelle the Conqueror 1988   ★ ★ ★ ★

Deeply moving Swedish drama about a widower, *Max Von Sydow*, and young son struggling to survive as immigrants in Denmark.

Pixote 1981   ★ ★ ★

Harrowing Brazilian exposé of plight of homeless children driven to crime, drugs and prostitution on the streets of Rio.

Playtime 1967   ★ ★ ★

Monsiuer Hulot finds himself in a futuristic Paris in Jacques Tati's comedy delight.

Ran 1985   ★ ★ ★ ★ ★

Stunning Japanese version of 'King Lear' by master movie-maker Akira Kurosawa.

Red Sorghum 1987

Evocative, moving story of two strong-minded Chinese in 1920's and 1930's. Rich in detail, visually spectacular.

Return of Martin Guerre, The 1982   ★ ★ ★

C16th French tale - based on fact - of villager, *GÇrard Depardieu*, returning home a changed character. But is he an impostor?

Rules of the Game, The 1939

Jean Renoir's tragi-comic masterpiece of love and intrigue among weekend house guests at a shooting party.

Salaam Bombay! 1988 ★ ★ ★
Vivid characterization marks potent Indian tale of young boy's struggle to survive on the streets of Bombay.

Seven Samurai, The 1954 ★ ★ ★ ★ ★
Akira Kurosawa masterpiece from which 'The Magnificent Seven' was taken. Must be on everyone's list of the ten best.

Seventh Seal, The 1957 ★ ★ ★ ★ ★
Magical, classic Swedish gem from Ingmar Bergman. A C14th Knight, Max Von Sydow, plays chess with death and gets an insight into life.

Subway 1985 ★ ★ ★
Stylish French movie about a thief, *Christopher Lambert*, hiding out among the strange community living in the Paris Metro.

Swann in Love 1984 ★ ★
Tightly squeezed excerpt from Prost's 'Remembrance of Thing's Past'. *Jeremy Irons* as French aristocrat consumed by passion for social-climbing *Ornella Muti*.

FOR

Tatie Danielle 1991 ★ ★ ★ ★
Delightful French comedy veers to the black as embittered widow, *Tsilla Chelton*, exorcises her anger on those around her.

Throne of Blood 1957 ★ ★ ★ ★
Akira Kurosawa's masterly adaptation of Macbeth in a Samurai setting. A truly great movie.

Toto The Hero 1991 (on video 92) ★ ★ ★ ★
Belgian comedy/drama. Elderly Toto, believing he was given to wrong parents, seeks revenge for lost, wasted life.

Trop Belle Pour Toi 1989 ★ ★
Gérard Depardieu in bitter-sweet tale of husband who chooses homely mistress over beautiful wife.

Women on the Verge of a Nervous Breakdown 1988 ★ ★ ★
Glamorous Spanish farce of a pregnant soap opera star dumped by her long-term lover.

American Werewolf in London, An 1981

Brilliant use of sound-track to indicate numerous changes of pace in cracking, tongue-in-cheek horror movie by John Landis.

Arachnaphobia 1990

Slick, Spielberg produced, comic thriller about small town overrun by killer spiders.

Birds, The 1963

Crows menace small-town America in Hitchcock horror unjaded by passage of time.

Blue Velvet 1986

David Lynch's stylish, distasteful story of small-town perversion and murder. *Dennis Hopper's* psycho sex-maniac steals show.

Boston Strangler, The 1968

Absorbing docudrama relates crimes, investigation and trial of the woman slayer, *Tony Curtis*.

Cape Fear 1991 (on video Autumn 92)

HOR

Robert De Niro seeks revenge on lawyer, *Nick Nolte*, and family in Martin Scorsese's violent, horrifying and brilliant movie.

Carrie 1976

Lonesome, creepy child, *Sissy Spacek*, unleashes telekinetic powers against those who wronged her. Shock-horror ending is screen classic.

Cat People 1982

Nastassia Kinski purrs in ineffectual horror of incest, bondage and bestiality.

Child's Play 1988

Sinister doll possessed by spirit of dead murderer in violent, sometimes amusing, chiller.

Fly, The 1986

Jeff Goldblum metamorphoses into irate bluebottle. Special effects and touches of humour make it a watchable horror.

Friday 13th 1980

Gory slasher-movie. Teenagers slaughtered in summer camp. Led to numerous, increasingly inept sequels.

Halloween 1978

John Carpenter's gripping chiller in which baby-sitter _Jamie Lee Curtis_ is terrorised by manic killer. Low-grade sequels followed.

Hellraiser 1987

Gruesome horror from Clive Barker notable for special effects.

Hills Have Eyes, The 1977

Cheap but effective tale about a family on a camping holiday persecuted by cannibals.

Hitcher The 1986

Rutger Hauer's haunting as the hitch-hiker preying on the drivers who give him a lift. Some extreme violence.

Howling, The 1981

Joe Dante's tongue-in-cheek story of Californian community overrun by werewolves. Led to several dreary sequels.

Misery 1990

Car crash leaves novelist, _James Caan,_ imprisoned by number one fan, _Kathy Bates,_ in exceptional psychological blood-curdler.

Nightmare on Elm Street, A 1984 ★ ★ ★

Wes Craven's teenage nightmare terrifies thanks to eerie effects and _Robert Englund_ as bogey man.

Omen, The 1976 ★ ★ ★ ★

Son of _Gregory Peck_ and _Lee Remick_ turns out to be Antichrist in gripping tale of the supernatural.

Paperhouse 1988 ★ ★

Engaging psychological study of pre-pubescent who enters imaginary world of her own drawings.

People Under the Stairs, The 1991 (on video Autumn 92)

Tongue-in-cheek horror from Wes Craven. Black child rescues little girl and other strange inmates from weird house.

Pet Sematary 1989

Family suffers all sorts of nastiness in new home behind Indian burial ground in Steven King nasty.

Poltergeist 1982

Scary goings-on when young girl is 'kidnapped' by spirits that have invaded her home.

Psycho 1960

Still the best of old shock-horror movies. _Anthony Perkins_ as demented Norman Bates in Hitchcock classic.

Rosemary's Baby 1968

Mia Farrow suffers psychological torment - and worse - when husband, _John Cassavetes_, becomes involved with Satanic cult.

Shining, The 1980

Jack Nicholson, caretaker at off-season hotel, goes mad in overlong but nevertheless underrated, Stanley Kubrick chiller based on Stephen King novel.

Silence of the Lambs, The 1991

Outstanding film. Rookie F.B.I. agent, Jodie Foster, hunts serial killer with help of incarcerated psychopath, _Anthony Hopkins_.

Tales from the Dark Side 1990

Christian Slater and _Debbie Harry_ contribute to four horror stories written by masters of the genre such as Conan Doyle and Stephen King.

Vampire's Kiss 1989 ⭐

Horror spoof which falls apart as publisher _Nicholas Cage_ imagines he's a vampire after lusty _Jennifer Beals_ bites him.

Woman in Black, The 1989 ⭐⭐⭐

Terrifying ghost story by novelist Susan Hill, cleverly adapted for TV.

All That Jazz 1979

Imaginative piece starring _Roy Scheider_ as choreographer Joe Gideon working himself into grave.

Amadeus 1984

Oscar-winning examination of rivalry between envious court composer Salieri (_F. Murray Abrahams_) and scatological young upstart Mozart (_Tom Hulce_).

American in Paris, An 1951

Gene Kelly, _Leslie Caron_ and Gershwin tunes in great musical spectacle.

Anchors Aweigh 1945

All-singing, all-dancing _Gene Kelly_ and _Frank Sinatra_ as a couple of sailors enjoying shore leave.

Band Wagon, The 1953

Backstage story with _Fred Astaire_, _Cyd Charisse_, _Jack Buchanan_ and the song 'That's Entertainment' among many others.

Barkleys of Broadway, The 1949

Final pairing of _Ginger Rogers_ and _Fred Astaire_, themselves reuniting after ten years, as showbiz couple who split up and reunite.

Blues Brothers, The 1980

John Landis cult comedy with _James Belushi_ and _Dan Akroyd_ as musicians trying to save an orphanage. Great score.

Brigadoon 1954

Twee but charming tale. _Gene Kelly_ the American finding mythical Scottish village and _Cyd Charisse_.

Buddy Holly Story, The 1978

Soundtrack's the star though _Gary Busey_ competent as ill-fated legendary singer.

Cabaret 1972

Liza Minelli leads first-rate movie set in pre-war Nazi Germany. Based on Christoper Isherwood stories.

Calamity Jane 1984 ★ ★

Doris Day gives up gun totin' for singin' in the wild west. _Howard Keel_ as Wild Bill Hickock.

Carmen 1984 ★ ★

Spanish staging of Bizet's opera with love affair between director and leading lady. Marvellous choreography.

Chuck Berry: Hail! Hail! Rock and Roll 1987 ★ ★

Documentary about the legendary old singer. A pretty candid look at his sometimes shocking life and times.

Commitments, The 1991 ★ ★ ★ ★

Alan Parker's funny, joyous story of a Dublin soul band.

Cover Girl 1944 ★ ★

Jolly but clichéd comedy with _Rita Hayworth_ and _Gene Kelly_, partly saved by Jerome Kern and Ira Gershwin score.

Dirty Dancing 1987 ★ ★ ★

Patrick Swayze hot-hoofs his way into _Jennifer Grey's_ heart in slim but pleasing rites-of-passage story.

Don't Look Back 1967 ★ ★

Closely observed documentary of _Bob Dylan's_ 1965 England tour. _Joan Baez, Donovan_ and _Alan Price_ also take part.

Doors, The 1991 ★ ★ ★

Oliver Stone's interesting version of the life of Jim Morrison _(Val Kilmer)_ and those around him.

Earth Girls are Easy 1989 ★

Vibrant colours and songs do little to help feeble comedy of three licentious aliens invading home of valley girl, _Geena Davis_.

Easter Parade 1948 ★ ★ ★

Lovely Irving Berlin score with _Fred Astaire, Judy Garland_ and _Ann Miller_ in showbiz setting.

Fame: The Movie 1980

New York school of performing arts is the setting for Alan Parker's attractive musical drama.

Fiddler on the Roof 1971

Nostalgic tale of a father, *Topol*, clinging to old Jewish values and trying to marry off his daughters in changing Russia.

Flashdance 1983

Young *Jennifer Beals* dreams of making the big time as a dancer in pretty daft Adrian Lyne movie, saved by dancing sequences.

42nd Street 1933

Set in 1933, this is the classic story of the understudy who comes back a star.

Funny Face 1957

Gershwin score enhances musical romance with *Fred Astaire* discovering talents of *Audrey Hepburn*.

Funny Girl 1968

Touching biopic with a roller-skating *Barbara Streisand* playing Ziegfield Follies star Fanny Brice.

Gentlemen Prefer Blondes 1953   **MUS**

Harold Hawkes musical comedy provides lightweight show-case for man-hungry *Marilyn Monroe* and *Jane Russell*.

Gigi 1958

'Thank heaven for little girls' - musical gem with ravishing *Leslie Caron* more interested in *Louis Jourdan* than becoming a courtesan.

Glenn Miller Story, The 1954 ★ ★ ★ ★

James Stewart's warm and convincing portrayal of the famed band leader.

Grease 1978 ★ ★

Bland story of young love enhanced by great Bee Gee songs and enthusiastic performances from *John Travolta* and *Olivia Newton John*.

Gypsy 1962

Natalie Wood and _Rosalind Russell_ star in entertaining biography of stripper Gypsy Rose Lee and her mum.

Hard Day's Night, A 1964

This day-in-the-life of a pop group was the best of _The Beatles_ comedy films.

Hello, Dolly! 1969

Gene Kelly directs _Barbara Streisand_ as a meddling matchmaker in period piece that doesn't reach expectations.

High Society 1956

Lovely musical version of 'The Philadelphia Story' with _Grace Kelly, Frank Sinatra, Bing Crosby_ and Cole Porter songs.

Holiday Inn 1942

Romantic tale notable for _Bing Crosby's_ rendition of 'White Christmas'. _Fred Astaire_ provides nifty footwork.

In Bed with Madonna 1991

Self-indulgent peep at musical megastar on tour. Concert footage redeems it.

Jesus Christ, Superstar 1973

Innovative Andrew Lloyd Webber and Tim Rice stage hit brought entertainingly to screen by Norman Jewison.

Jolson Story, The 1946

Jolson sings but _Larry Parks_ acts in biopic of the great vaudeville/Broadway singer.

King and I, The 1956

Rogers and Hammerstein charmer set in court of Siam. Governess, _Deborah Kerr_, instructs royal children and falls for King, _Yul Brynner_.

Kiss Me Kate 1953

Great Cole Porter frolic loosely based on 'The Taming of the Shrew'. _Ann Miller, Howard Keel_ and _Ann Blyth_ on brilliant form.

La Bamba 1987   ★ ★

Competent biopic about popster Ritchie Valens who made the fatal mistake of hitching a ride in Buddy Holly's plane.

Little Shop of Horrors, The 1986   ★ ★ ★

Mixed genres of horror, comedy and music spark mixed reaction to Frank Oz's movie. *Rick Moranis, Steve Martin* and *Bill Murray* among the cast.

Meet Me in St Louis 1944   ★ ★ ★

Heartwarming *Judy Garland* vehicle based on a year in the life of a family during the St. Louis World Fair, 1903.

Merry Widow, The 1934   ★ ★

Maurice Chevalier and *Jeanette MacDonald* belt out smashing numbers in rich film version of Franz Lehar's operetta.

Mo' Better Blues 1990   ★ ★

Spike Leigh's backstage look at a jazz musician, *Denzel Washington*, and the women in his life.

Music Man, The 1962   ★ ★

Tuneful tale about salesman-cum-con artist, *Robert Preston*, who arrives in small town to form a brass band.

My Fair Lady 1964   ★ ★ ★   **MUS**

Audrey Hepburn as the Victorian flower-girl turned into a lady by professor, *Rex Harrison*. Lovely score, design and costumes.

New York, New York 1977   ★ ★

Saxophonist, *Robert De Niro*, and singer, *Liza Minelli*, love and squabble through Big Band era in Scorsese's overlong, over-ambitious movie.

Oklahoma! 1955   ★ ★ ★

Rogers and Hammerstein again. *Shirley Jones* the country girl pursued by cowboy, *Gordon MacRae*, and evil farm-hand, *Rod Steiger*.

Oliver! 1968   ★ ★ ★ ★

Lavish musical version of 'Oliver Twist'. *Mark Lester* cute as Oliver; *Ron Moody* splendid as Fagin. Great score and choreography.

On the Town 1949   ★ ★

Exuberant yarn about sailors, *Gene Kelly* and *Frank Sinatra*, on 24-hour leave finding romance and adventure in New York.

Paint your Wagon 1969   ★ ★

Nice looking musical western. *Lee Marvin* and *Clint Eastwood* buy the same wife, *Jean Seberg*, at auction.

Pajama Game, The 1957   ★ ★ ★

Rousing romance with *Doris Day* heading factory workers' demands for pay rise but falling for boss.

Pal Joey 1957   ★ ★

Charming, libidinous heel, *Frank Sinatra*, uses women, *Kim Novak* and *Rita Hayworth*, in bid to build his own night club. Great songs, slim story.

Pennies from Heaven 1981   ★

Dennis Potter's British melodrama with music set during the depression. Flops when transposed to America.

Pink Floyd: The Wall 1982   ★ ★

Alan Parker's affectionate visualisation of the band's best-selling album. *Bobs Hoskins* and *Geldof* appear.

Pirate, The 1948   ★ ★

Judy Garland dreams of meeting famous pirate. Dashing *Gene Kelly* grants her wish.

Quadrophenia 1979   ★ ★

Mods and Rockers fight it out on Britain's beaches. *Sting* makes strong impression in acting debut.

Rocky Horror Picture Show, The 1975   ★ ★ ★

Avant garde rock romp which achieved cult status for it's vampish look.

Round Midnight 1986   ★ ★

Bertrand Tavernier's loving homage to the great jazz musicians, Bud Powell and Lester Young. Nice score from Herbie Hancock.

Saturday Night Fever 1977   ★ ★ ★

Catchy tunes, nice dance numbers and a plot about an ambitious young Italian, *John Travolta*, make for agreeable entertainment.

Seven Brides for Seven Brothers 1954   ★ ★ ★ ★

Delightful songs plus some of the best choreography ever staged. *Jane Powell* the young bride making home for *Howard Keel* and his six brothers.

Show Boat 1951   ★ ★ ★ ★

Splendid weepy set on the Mississippi. Heartbreak and romance for *Howard Keel, Jane Grayson* and *Ava Gardner* to the strains of Jerome Kern's beautiful score.

Singin' in the Rain 1952   ★ ★ ★ ★ ★

Quite simply the best of all musicals. Great dancing by *Gene Kelly* and *Donald O'Connor*.

Sound of Music, The 1965   ★ ★ ★ ★

Sentimental saga of a nun, *Julie Andrews*, becoming nanny to large family in pre-war Austria. Wonderful songs.

South Pacific 1958   ★ ★ ★

Exotic Rogers and Hammerstein musical of WWII life on a pacific island. Songs include 'Nothing Like a Dame' and 'Happy Talk'.

That'll be the Day 1974   ★ ★ ★

Young lads in 1950's England use rock music to escape their humdrum lives. *David Essex* and *Ringo Starr*.

That's Entertainment pt 1 1974   ★ ★ ★

A loving eulogy of the best of M.G.M.'s musicals narrated by its stars and featuring a montage of the studio's greatest hits.

This is Spinal Tap 1984   ★ ★ ★

Wicked parody of rock-bands and music documentaries. Narrated and directed by Rob Reiner.

Top Hat 1935   ★ ★ ★

Wonderful songs and nifty footwork lift the usual, mistaken-identity plot in *Fred Astaire* and *Ginger Rogers* romance.

U2 Rattle and Hum 1988　　　　

Okay documentary about the celebrated Irish rock group on tour.

West Side Story 1961　　　　

Romeo and Juliet set to music in modern-day, gangland America. *Natalie Wood* and *Richard Beymer* the lovers from opposing gangs.

White Christmas 1954　　　　

Army pals, *Bing Crosby* and *Danny Kaye*, hired to boost popularity of holiday resort, aided by Irving Berlin's score.

Wizard of Oz, The 1939　　　　

Shirley Temple was initial choice for Dorothy but mercifully *Judy Garland* stepped into the ruby slippers for this enchanting fantasy musical.

Woodstock 1970　　　　★ ★

Seminal documentary of the famous weekend rock festival. Great footage of *The Who, Jimmy Hendrix, Joe Cocker, Sly and The Family Stone* amongst others.

Yankee-Doodle Dandy 1942　　　　★ ★ ★

James Cagney great as song and dance man-cum playwright, George M. Cohan, in lavish biography.

Absence of Malice 1981

Journalist, _Sally Field_, duped into writing story that discredits innocent and angry _Paul Newman_. Crisp melodrama.

Anderson Tapes, The 1972

Fast-moving thriller in which _Sean Connery_ attempts to pull off major heist under police surveillance.

Angel Heart 1987

Heartstopping tension from Alan Parker. _Mickey Rourke_ takes on _Robert De Niro_ as the devil in a suspense story not for the faint-hearted.

Basic Instinct 1992 (on video Winter 92)

Michael Douglas and _Sharon Stone_ in violent anti-feminist thriller with women shown as objects of fantasy or fear.

Bedroom Window, The 1987

Intriguing though over-plotted thriller. _Steve Guttenberg_ and _Elizabeth McGovern_ unwittingly involved in murder investigation.

Bellman and True 1988

Realistic suspense story of computer expert forced to aid robbery when son is kidnapped.

Best Seller 1987

Uneasy - but engaging - alliance of author/cop, _Brian Dennehey_, appointed by hitman, _James Woods_, stirs up viper's nest of corruption.

Big Easy, The 1987 ★ ★ ★

Offbeat, New Orleans cop, _Dennis Quaid_, and uptight but sexy D.A., _Ellen Barkin_, investigate case of police corruption.

Big Sleep, The 1944 ★ ★ ★ ★ ★

Howard Hawks directs _Humphrey Bogart_ and _Lauren Bacall_ in Philip Marlowe investigation of sex and murder. Confusing but terrific.

Black Widow 1986 ★ ★

F.B.I. agent, _Debra Winger_, seduced by wealthy suspect, _Theresa Russell_. Lots of twists keep it moving at rapid pace.

Blade Runner 1982   ★ ★ ★

Impressive, futuristic thriller in which cop, _Harrison Ford_, tracks down escaped robots _Rutger Hauer, Sean Young_ and _Darryl Hannah_.

Blood Simple 1984   ★ ★

John Getz hires private eye _Emmett Walsh_ to spy on wife in Coen brothers' much-admired, deeply flawed film debut.

Blow Out 1981   ★ ★

Brian de Palma's sexy thriller about a soundman, _John Travolta_, innocently taping a murder.

Blue Desert 1991 (on video Summer 92)   ★

Danger for _D.B. Sweeney_ in Nevada-based crime story.

Body Heat 1981   ★ ★ ★

Lawrence Kasdan's sweaty, erotic conspiracy in which _William Hurt_ and _Kathleen Turner_ plot to kill her husband.

Brighton Rock 1947   ★ ★ ★

Excellent adaptation of Grahame Greene's psychological thriller. _Richard Attenborough_ as Pinkie.

Cape Fear 1991 (on video Autumn 92)   ★ ★ ★ ★

Robert De Niro seeks revenge on lawyer, _Nick Nolte_, and family in Martin Scorsese's violent, horrifying and brilliant movie.

Cat and the Canary, The 1978   ★ ★

Period whodunit in spooky mansion housing _Bob Hope_ and _Paulette Goddard_ among others.

China Syndrome, The 1979   ★ ★ ★

Accident at nuclear power station and subsequent cover up provide meaty roles for _Jane Fonda_ and _Michael Douglas_.

Chinatown 1974   ★ ★ ★ ★ ★

Faye Dunaway hires private eye, _Jack Nicholson_, in tense, riveting mystery set in 1930's L.A.. A modern classic.

Company Business 1991

Two veteran spies, *Gene Hackman* and *Mikhail Baryshnikov*, forced on the run in mediocre suspense drama.

Conversation, The 1974

Excellent Francis Coppolla story of surveillance operator, *Gene Hackman*, becoming personally involved in case of murder.

Criminal Law 1989

Weakly plotted story of attorney's dilemma when his acquitted client plans to kill again. With *Gary Oldman* and *Kevin Bacon*.

Day of the Jackal, The 1973

Suspenseful political drama sees *Edward Fox* as cunning assassin gunning for French president.

Dead Again 1991 (on video Autumn 92)

Complex, intriguing plot providing dual roles for husband and wife team, *Emma Thompson* and *Kenneth Branagh*.

Dead Calm 1989

Mystery and mayhem aboard hijacked yacht. *Billy Zane* steals the scene as psycho killer.

Deadly Affair, The 1967

Sidney Lumet's web of espionage starring *James Mason*, based on Le Carré novel.

Deadly Pursuit 1988

Killer at large in mountain expedition led by *Kirsty Alley* pursued by detective *Sidney Poitier* and *Tom Berenger*.

Deceived 1991 (on video Autumn 92)

Goldie Hawn discovering to her peril her husband's deception and double life. Nicely done.

Defence of the Realm 1985

Government cover-up forms basis of British political conspiracy and murder with *Gabriel Byrne* and *Denholm Elliot*.

Dial M for Murder 1954

Alfred Hitchcock at his most teasing; *Ray Milland* the conniving husband of tormented *Grace Kelly*.

D.O.A. 1988

When *Dennis Quaid* discovers he's been poisoned with only 24 hours to live, he and *Meg Ryan* go after the killer.

Dog Day Afternoon 1975

Al Pacino terrific as loser who robs bank so lover can have sex-change op. But raid goes disastrously wrong.

Don't Look Now 1973

Julie Christie and *Donald Sutherland* haunted by visions of dead daughter in Nicholas Roeg's much-admired psychological thriller.

Dressed to Kill 1980

Brian de Palma's sexy, sometimes distasteful thriller has killer stalking *Angie Dickinson* and *Nancy Allen*. *Michael Caine* stars.

Duel 1971

Tense stuff as mild motorist, *Dennis Weaver*, is persecuted by oil-truck driver. Steven Spielberg's first film.

Everybody Wins 1990

Nick Nolte and *Debra Winger* in convoluted Arthur Miller plot try to clear young boy of murder charge.

Fatal Attraction 1987

Glenn Close as obsessed, spurned mistress wreaking revenge on *Michael Douglas* and family. Gripping but overblown.

Fatal Vision 1984

Murder mystery based on true story of American doctor accused of murdering wife and daughters. *Karl Malden* splendid as man seeking justice.

Femme Fatale 1991 (on video Summer 92)

Newlywed's wife mysteriously vanishes in thriller starring *Billy Zane* and *Colin Firth*.

Frantic 1988

★★

Hit and miss mystery by Roman Polanski in which *Harrison Ford* and *Emmanuelle Seigne* search Paris for his missing wife.

Funeral in Berlin 1966

★★

Sequel to 'The Ipcress File'. *Michael Caine* reprises role of Harry Parker in sharp spy drama.

FX: Murder by Illusion 1986

★

Fast-paced caper about special effects man hired to protect a supergrass. *Bryan Brown* and *Brian Dennehey* star.

Gorky Park 1983

★★★

Intriguing spy story set in the last days of the cold war. With *William Hurt*.

Homicide 1991

★★★

Jewish cop, *Joe Mantegna*, finds his loyalties divided when he investigates sinister murder of Jewish pawn shop owner.

Hot Spot, The 1990

★★

Steamy and atmospheric conspiracy story. *Don Johnson* and *Virginia Madsen* as ne'er do wells who deserve each other in hot southern town.

House of Games 1987

★★

David Mamet's ingenious tale of psychiatrist embroiled in web of mystery when she helps a con-man patient.

Hunt for Red October, The 1990

★★★

Exciting suspense thriller about a Soviet Captain, *Sean Connery*, using a state-of-the-art submarine to defect.

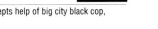

MYS/
THR

In the Heat of the Night 1967

★★★★

Bigoted southern sheriff, *Rod Steiger*, grudgingly accepts help of big city black cop, *Sidney Poitier*, in murder investigation.

Ipcress File, The 1965

★★★

Michael Caine's first and best outing as Len Deighton's Cockney secret agent, Harry Palmer.

Jacob's Ladder 1990   ★ ★

Psychological drama with *Tim Robbins* as Vietnam vet discovering source of his terrifying hallucinations.

Jagged Edge 1985   ★ ★ ★ ★

Excellent, tense, did-he-didn't-he suspense thriller. Lawyer, *Glenn Close*, defends *Jeff Bridges*, accused of murdering his wife.

Kiss Before Dying, A 1991   ★

Psychopath *Matt Dillon* uses wife, *Sean Young*, to achieve greedy ambitions. Poor remake of goodish 1956 movie.

Klute 1971   ★ ★ ★ ★

Jane Fonda a prostitute pestered by psycho. *Donald Sutherland* the helpful cop. Tense, first-rate thriller.

Laura 1944

Ever-popular whodunnit. *Gene Tierney* the supposed victim with whose picture detective, *Dana Andrews*, falls in love.

Legal Eagles 1986

Not bad mystery teams D.A., *Robert Redford*, lawyer, *Debra Winger* and her flaky client, *Darryl Hannah*, on murder trail.

Looking for Mr Goodbar 1977

Glum, sordid tale of repressed young woman, *Diane Keaton*, seeking sex - and danger - in singles bar.

Love at Large 1990

Thin comic thriller. P.I., *Tom Berenger*, hired by mysterious *Anne Archer*, discovers he's being shadowed by another P.I., *Elizabeth Perkins*.

Maltese Falcon, The 1941

Classic, evergreen film noir from John Huston. Great performances by *Humphrey Bogart* (as Sam Spade), *Sidney Greenstreet, Peter Lorre* and *Mary Astor*.

Manhunter 1986   ★ ★

Troubled F.B.I. agent, *William Petersen*, must think like a serial killer to catch one. First screen appearance of Hannibal Lecter (*Brian Cox*).

Missing 1982

Excellent political thriller about a father, *Jack Lemmon*, trying to uncover mystery surrounding his son's disappearance in Chile.

Mister Frost 1990

Stodgy Europudding in which *Jeff Goldblum* plays cold-blooded killer, convinced he's the devil.

Mona Lisa 1986

London underworld provides the backdrop for romantic thriller with *Bob Hoskins, Cathy Tyson* and *Michael Caine*.

Morning After, The 1986

Disappointing considering Sidney Lumet directs. *Jane Fonda* wakes up next to a mysterious dead man. *Jeff Bridges* helps solve the problem.

Mortal Thoughts 1991

Two women attempt to cover up the murder of a brutish husband, *Bruce Willis*. Stylish but uninvolving.

Murder on the Orient Express 1974

Albert Finney as Hercule Poirot, solving murder aboard train.

Music Box, The 1989

Costa-Gavras' powerful story of lawyer, *Jessica Lange*, defending father accused of wartime atrocities.

Night of the Hunter 1955   ★ ★ ★

Robert Mitchum as psychotic preacher on the prowl. Suspenseful examination of good and evil. Only film Charles Laughton directed.

MYS/ THR

Night to Remember, A 1943   ★ ★ ★

Mystery writer and wife, *Brian Aherne* and *Loretta Young*, investigate murder in lively comedy/thriller.

North by Northwest 1959   ★ ★ ★

Sparkling Hitchcock adventure with *Cary Grant* as innocuous advertising executive mistaken for spy.

Notorious 1946

Romantic Hitchcock thriller set in Rio and involving *Cary Grant, Ingrid Bergman* and Nazi plots.

No Way Out 1987

Sex, suspense, murder and cover-up within U.S. Government. *Kevin Costner, Gene Hackman* and *Sean Young* in ménage-à-trois.

Pacific Heights 1990

Psychological battle as ex-lodger, *Michael Keaton*, persecutes landlords, *Melanie Griffith* and *Matthew Modine*.

Package, The 1989

Gene Hackman becomes the fall guy in east-west conspiracy while conducting prisoner, *Tommy Lee Jones*, to Washington.

Paper Mask 1990

Originally interesting, ultimately silly plot of hospital porter, *Paul McGann*, successfully posing as doctor.

Parallax View, The 1974

Warren Beatty stars in intriguing conspiracy theory tale reminiscent of John Kennedy assassination.

Peeping Tom 1960   ★ ★ ★

Once controversial, Michael Powell shocker about a psychopath who photographs his victims as he kills them.

Performance 1970   ★ ★

Hunted criminal, *James Fox*, and rock musician, *Mick Jagger*, find their lives intertwine. Odd but interesting.

Play Misty for Me 1971   ★ ★ ★ ★

Spurned lover, *Jessica Walter*, obsessively seeks revenge on D.J., *Clint Eastwood*. This is 'Fatal Attraction' but earlier and better.

Presumed Innocent 1990

Gripping did-he, didn't-he story about an attorney, *Harrison Ford*, suspected when girlfriend murdered.

Prime Suspect 1982

Adequate, made-for-TV movie in which an innocent member of public is persecuted after young girl's murder.

Private Life of Sherlock Holmes, The 1970

Billy Wilder's affectionate look at hitherto unknown aspects of the great detective's career. With _Robert Stevens_ and _Colin Blakely_.

Prizzi's Honour 1985

Blackly comic Mafia movie in which rival hit-persons, _Jack Nicholson_ and _Kathleen Turner_, fall in love.

Psycho 1960

Still the best of old shock-horror movies. _Anthony Perkins_ as demented Norman Bates in Hitchcock classic.

Q and A 1990

Intelligent investigation of deep-rooted corruption within N.Y. police force. _Nick Nolte_ the bent copper; _Timothy Hutton_ the crusading D.A..

Rear Window 1954

Hitchcock at his most stylish. Incapacitated _James Stewart_ witnesses murder across the street. _Grace Kelly_ helps him investigate.

Rebecca 1940

Daphne Du Maurier's romantic saga of young bride haunted by memory of husband's first wife. With _Joan Fontaine_ and _Laurence Olivier_.

Ricochet 1992 (on video Autumn 92)

Predictable story of a psychopath hunting the man who imprisoned him. _Denzel Washington_ and _John Lithgow_ star.

Sea of Love 1989 ★★★★

Scintillating, sexy thriller with _Al Pacino_ investigating a series of murders. and falling for chief suspect, _Ellen Barkin_.

Sleeping with the Enemy 1991 ★

Murderous husband, _Patrick Bergin_, hunting runaway wife, _Julia Roberts_, in dreary tale.

MYS/ THR

Society 1989

`★`

Teenage mystery, merely worth mentioning for shocking special effects, everything else is bland and dull.

Someone to Watch Over Me 1987

`★ ★ ★ ★`

Sensational blend of romance and suspense as married policeman, _Tom Berenger_, falls in love with witness he's protecting, _Mimi Rogers_.

Spellbound 1945

`★ ★ ★`

Hitchcock's psychological drama of psychoanalyst, _Ingrid Bergman_, falling in love with her boss, _Gregory Peck_, while unravelling his problems as a patient.

Stage Fright 1950

`★ ★`

Disappointing Hitchcock offering about a drama student, _Richard Todd_, framed for murder.

Stakeout 1987

`★ ★ ★`

Witty thriller in which policeman, _Richard Dreyfuss_, falls for the woman, _Madeleine Stowe_, he's meant to be watching. _Emilio Estevez_ is his disapproving partner.

Strangers on a Train 1951

`★ ★ ★`

Snappy Hitchcock direction. _Farley Granger_ and _Robert Walker_ exchange murders to avoid suspicion.

Suspect 1987

`★ ★ ★ ★`

Intriguing suspense thriller about a lawyer, _Cher_, defending deaf mute, _Liam Neeson_, on a murder charge, with the illegal help of juror, _Dennis Quaid_.

Sweet Revenge 1987

Kelly McGillis and _Alec Baldwin_ in story of woman out to get own back on someone who did her and her brother wrong.

Taking of Pelham 123, The 1974

`★ ★ ★`

Robert Shaw hijacks a New York subway train, holding the passengers to ransom. _Walter Matthau_ has a tension-packed hour to free them.

Taxi Driver 1976

Martin Scorsese's disturbing but brilliant view of ultra-violent New York seen through the eyes of a psychotic cabbie, _Robert De Niro_.

Thirty Nine Steps, The 1935   ★ ★ ★ ★

Cracking tale of murder espionage and romance. Hitchcock directs, *Robert Donat* and *Madeline Carroll* star. Another classic.

Thomas Crown Affair, The 1968   ★ ★ ★ ★

Sharp, sexy thriller; *Steve McQueen*, a gentleman bank robber, *Faye Dunaway*, the insurance investigator out to catch him.

To Catch a Killer 1991   ★ ★

Brian Dennehey flexes his acting muscles in a one man fight to bring a mass murderer to justice.

To Catch a Thief 1955   ★ ★

Fun and suspense from Hitchcock. Retired cat-burglar, *Cary Grant*, suspected of recent robberies on French Riviera, tracks down the real culprit. *Grace Kelly* the wealthy love interest.

Touch and Die 1990   ★ ★

American journalist investigates a series of murders in Europe. *Martin Sheen* and youngest offspring, *Renee Estevez*, do the honours.

Trouble with Harry, The 1955   ★ ★ ★

Off-beat Hitchcock comedy/thriller about problems of disposing of a corpse. Stars *John Forsyth* before his hair turned blue in 'Dynasty'.

Turner and Hooch 1989   ★ ★

Entertaining comedy/thriller concerning one cop, *Tom Hanks*, and his dog.

Two Jakes, The 1990   ★

Disappointing sequel to 'Chinatown'. *Jack Nicholson* stars and directs but still can't make it work.

Vertigo 1958   ★ ★

Flawed but enjoyable Hitchcock mystery with *James Stewart* as ex-cop hired to keep an eye on friend's wife, *Kim Novak*.

V.I. Warshawski 1991   ★

Kathleen Turner does her best as wise-cracking private eye but the film falls flat.

MYS/
THR

White Nights 1985

Thriller starring *Gregory Hines* and Russian ballet star, *Mikhail Baryshnikov*, planning to defect from U.S.S.R. to America.

Wicker Man, The 1973

Palm-sweating tale about a Scottish policeman, *Edward Woodward*, investigating the disappearance of child on eerie island.

Witness 1985

Magnetic combination of action, romance, suspense and thrills. Cop, *Harrison Ford*, uncovers high level corruption while hiding out with murder witness in the Amish community.

Witness for the Prosecution 1957

Agatha Christie plot expertly adapted by Billy Wilder. Good performances by *Charles Laughton*, *Marlene Dietrich* and *Tyrone Power*.

Alien 1979

★★★★

Terrifying galaxy adventure of epic proportions aboard a plagued spaceship. *Sigourney Weaver, Tom Skerritt* and *John Hurt* excellent. Breath-taking special effects.

Aliens 1986

★★★

Not as good as original. More violence than plot but still exciting stuff.

Altered States 1980

★★

Roller-coaster psychological study of scientist, *William Hurt*. Directed flamboyantly by Ken Russell.

Back to the Future 1985

★★★★

Michael J. Fox sent to the past to ensure his future in a terrific movie. First and best of the series.

Back to the Future II 1989

★★

Too fast, too complex, too harsh sequel has Fox and nutty professor, *Christopher Lloyd*, zipping through time like yo-yos.

Back to the Future III 1990

★★★

Back on form, *Fox* and *Lloyd* find themselves in the wild west where *Lloyd* finds romance.

Barbarella 1968

★★

Pre-feminist *Jane Fonda* explodes onto the screen as sexy adventuress leched over by inhabitants of strange C41st planet.

Batman 1989

★★★

Michael Keaton's moody hero overshadowed by *Jack Nicholson's* hammy Joker. Dark and impressive sets.

Batteries Not Included 1987

★

Aliens help poverty-stricken oldies battle to keep their home in thin extra-terrestrial comedy.

SCI/
FAN

Blade Runner 1982

★★★

Impressive, futuristic thriller in which cop, *Harrison Ford*, tracks down escaped robots *Rutger Hauer, Sean Young* and *Darryl Hannah*.

Brazil 1985

Terry Gilliam's futuristic social satire with *Robert De Niro, Jonathon Pryce* and *Bob Hoskins* achieved cult status in America.

Close Encounters of the Third Kind 1977

Fantastic Spielberg sci-fi about non-threatening aliens landing in America.

Cocoon 1985

Florida oldies find the fountain of youth, courtesy of visiting aliens, in warm, sentimental fable.

Company of Wolves, The 1984

Freudian but unsatisfying adult version of Little Red Riding Hood.

Dark Crystal, The 1983

Jim Henson's dark, superbly animated fable of good and evil.

Darkman, The 1990

Violence proves no substitute for plot in feeble thriller of disfigured scientist, *Liam Neeson*, wreaking revenge.

Empire Strikes Back, The 1980

Great action-packed sequel to Star Wars reuniting cast and crew with added special effects.

E.T. the Extra-Terrestrial 1982

The greatest fantasy movie ever about a little boy and his friendship with a stranded alien. Spielberg's direction quite superb.

Fantastic Voyage 1966

Miniaturized medical team (including *Raquel Welch*), on journey through scientist's bloodstream to save his life.

Field of Dreams 1989

Perfectly enchanting fantasy of a farmer, *Kevin Costner*, told by a disembodied voice to build baseball pitch in middle of crops so that late, great players may return. Magical.

Flash Gordon 1980

Comic strip hero bought to life by *Sam J. Jones*, in lavish sci-fi adventure. Good designs, score, supporting cast.

Freejack 1991 (on video Autumn 92)

Emilio Estevez and *Mick Jagger* lead mindless futuristic adventure about a man pulled into the next century.

Ghostbusters 1984

Who you gonna call if plagued by ghosts? *Dan Akroyd, Harold Ramis* and *Bill Murray*. Rib-tickling comedy with scary special effects.

Ghostbusters II 1989

Old gang return with fewer laughs, more violence as they battle a New Year's Eve explosion of spirits.

Gremlins 1984

Cute little creatures turn vicious if fed after midnight in adult children's story from the Spielberg stable.

Gremlins 2: The New Batch 1990

Effects are an improvement on original but story's weaker.

Highlander 1986

Action-adventure pairing immortal C16th *Sean Connery* and modern day pupil, *Christopher Lambert*.

Iceman 1984

Prehistoric man is alive and well and living in Antarctica where he's discovered by *Timothy Hutton*.

Innerspace 1987

Astronaut, *Dennis Quaid*, miniaturized and accidentally injected into hypochondriac, *Martin Short*. Fast and funny.

SCI/ FAN

Invasion of the Bodysnatchers 1956

Effective old horror of unfriendly aliens taking over bodies of town's inhabitants. (1978 remake also not bad.)

Jason and the Argonauts 1963   ★ ★ ★

Harryhausen special effects dominate legendary adventure of search for the Golden Fleece.

My Stepmother is an Alien 1988   ★ ★

Scientist, *Dan Aykroyd,* involved in comic capers when he marries extra-terrestrial, *Kim Bassinger.*

Nukie 1992   ★

Two cute aliens separated on Earth are reunited by African children.

Peggy Sue Got Married 1986   ★ ★

'Back To The Future' yarn. Disillusioned *Kathleen Turner,* given chance to return to high school and change her life.

Planet of the Apes 1968   ★ ★

American astronaut lands in future world populated by hostile apes. Humerous adventure with *Charlton Heston.*

Predator 1987   ★ ★

Arnold Schwarzenegger heads S.W.A.T team on rescue mission in jungle, but someone - or something - keeps killing them.

Repo Man 1984   ★ ★

Veteran car-repossessor, *Harry Dean Stanton,* shows rookie, *Emilio Estevez,* how to do it. Off-beat satire.

Return of the Jedi 1983   ★ ★ ★ ★

Final part of Star Wars trilogy, with Luke Skywalker and co. up against giant Deathstar. Special effects great as ever.

Short Circuit 1986   ★ ★

A cutesy robot comes to life to the surprise of its creator, *Steve Guttenberg.* Acceptable, sci-fi comedy.

Starman 1984   ★ ★

Jeff Bridges, an appealing alien who abducts widow, *Karen Allen,* to help him locate his spaceship.

Star Trek: The Motion Picture 1979   ★ ★

Disappointing film version of the marvellous TV series. Starship Enterprise crew battle to save earth from threatening force field. Star Trek's II, III and V not up to much.

Star Trek IV: The Voyage Home 1986   ★ ★ ★

Ecological message as the Enterprise land on C20th Earth to save the whales.

Star Trek VI: The Undiscovered Country 1991 (on video Autumn 92)   ★ ★ ★ ★

Best and final adventure of the old guard (*Shatner et al*). Enterprise must escort implacable enemies, the Klingons, to Inter-Galactic peace conference. Chaos ensues.

Star Wars 1977   ★ ★ ★ ★ ★

Marvellous classic sci-fi adventure. *Mark Hamill, Harrison Ford, Carrie Fisher, Alec Guinness* and robots (R2D2, C-3PO), in hugely imaginative Inter-Galactic western.

Superman 1978 and **II** 1980   ★ ★ ★

Much as you'd expect. *Christopher Reeve* as Superman, *Margot Kidder* as Lois Lane and such assorted villains as *Gene Hackman, Terence Stamp* and *Richard Pryor*.

Superman III 1983 and **IV** 1987   ★ ★

The mixture pretty much as before.

Terminator, The 1984   ★ ★ ★ ★

Robot, *Arnold Schwarzenegger*, sent back from future to stop mother-to-be, *Sarah Hamilton*, from giving birth to future saviour. Special effects and stunts the real stars.

Terminator 2 1991   ★ ★ ★ ★

Arnie's back - this time as a goody protecting *Hamilton* and her son from evil Cyborg. Story takes back seat to special effects even better than in the original.

Time Bandits, The 1981   ★ ★ ★ ★

SCI/
FAN

Ralph Richardson and six dwarfs escort young boy through time in hilarious romp with a cast of glittering guest stars. *Ian Holm* marvellous as tiny Napoleon.

Timescape 1991   ★

Small-town America visited by group from the future who offer widower, *Jeff Daniels*, a new life.

Total Recall 1990

Arnold Schwarzenegger provides the brawn, special effects the brain in violent futuristic thriller in which technology can inject memories into minds.

Toxic Avenger, The 1985

Souffle-light spoof on comic strip heros. Not to everyone's taste but generally pleasing.

2001: A Space Odyssey 1968

Stanley Kubrick's ground-breaking account of a space journey, jeopardized when the computer takes control.

War of the Worlds, The 1953

Martians invade; *Gene Barry* and *Les Tremayne* star in commendable version of H.G. Wells story. Oscar-winning special effects.

Westworld 1973

Ambitious thriller set in a future where a Disneyland for adults is staffed by robots.

When Worlds Collide 1951 ★ ★

Corny, end-of-the-world fable distinguished by Oscar-winning special effects.

Willow 1988 ★ ★

Fantasy adventure of a dwarf guarding a baby saviour with the help of *Val Kilmer* and *Joanne Whalley-Kilmer*.

Alamo, The 1960

John Wayne's long, earnest version of America's Dunkirk-like defeat in the old west.

Big Country, The 1958

Pleasing direction from William Wyler. City man, _Gregory Peck_, shown country ways by _Jean Simmons_ and _Charlton Heston_.

Buffalo Bill and the Indians 1976

Robert Altman's quirky look at Buffalo Bill's entertainment empire with _Paul Newman_ and _Burt Lancaster_.

Butch Cassidy and the Sundance Kid 1969

Unbeatable romantic, funny, action western. Inspired pairing of _Paul Newman_ and _Robert Redford_ as lawless buddies.

Cat Ballou 1965

Comic action/adventure sees _Jane Fonda_ and a drunken _Lee Marvin_ avenging her father's death.

Cheyenne Autumn 1964

John Ford's last, oddly pessimistic, account of Cheyenne tribe's journey back to original settlement.

Cowboys, The 1972

John Wayne forced to take group of young boys on cattle drive in slow, earnest story.

Dances with Wolves 1990

Oscar-winning directorial debut by star _Kevin Costner_ - in post-civil war epic .

Duel in the Sun 1946

King Vidor western with _Gregory Peck_ and _Joseph Cotton_ fighting over half-breed, _Jennnifer Jones_. Sometimes known as 'Lust in the Dust'.

Fistful of Dollars, A 1964

'Man with no name' _Clint Eastwood_ blows into old west town torn apart by feud. Stylish spaghetti western.

WES

For a Few Dollars More 1967

Bounty hunters, *Lee Van Cleef* and the laconic *Clint Eastwood*, in violent sequel to 'A Fistful of Dollars'.

Fort Apache 1948

Deliberately paced by John Ford action/drama revolving around conflict between martinet cavalry officer, *Henry Fonda*, and pragmatic subordinate, *John Wayne*.

Good, the Bad and the Ugly, The 1967

Clint Eastwood 'The Good', *Lee Van Cleef* 'The Bad' and *Eli Wallach's* 'The Ugly' in top-rate spaghetti western.

Harley Davidson and the Marlboro Man 1991

Don Johnson and *Mickey Rourke* feature in a poor contemporary western.

High Noon 1952

Classic adventure with *Gary Cooper* the sheriff single-handedly facing the vengeful bad guys on Main Street.

High Plains Drifter 1973

Mystical western with *Clint Eastwood* as avenging angel cleaning up corrupt town.

How the West was Won 1962

Spectacular saga covering three generations. Narrated by *Spencer Tracy* and starring horde of great screen cowboys; *Wayne, Peck, Stewart, Fonda, Widmark* etc..

Jeremiah Johnson 1972

Rambling, occasionally gripping, tale of mountain man, *Robert Redford*, surviving the wilderness.

Jesse James 1939

Colourful, romanticized version of life of notorious outlaw. *Tyrone Power* as Jesse, *Henry Fonda* as brother Frank.

Left-Handed Gun, The 1958

First method western. Psychological study of exploits of Billy the Kid (*Paul Newman*).

Little Big Man 1970   ★ ★ ★ ★

Epic, sprawling saga focusing upon the reminiscences of a 120-year-old half-breed, *Dustin Hoffman*.

Magnificent Seven, The 1960   ★ ★ ★ ★ ★

Smashing adaptation of Kurosawa's 'The Seven Samurai'. Hired guns protect Mexican village from gang of bandits. *Yul Brynner, Steve McQueen, Charles Bronson* et al.. Excellent.

Major Dundee 1965   ★ ★ ★

Sam Peckinpah directed this disturbing drama of confederate pioneers sent to quell the Apaches.

Man Called Horse, A 1970   ★ ★

Gory but gripping study of Sioux culture. Captured *Richard Harris* undergoes torture to prove manhood.

Man from Laramie, The 1955   ★ ★ ★ ★

Absorbing *James Stewart* western sees him out for revenge when his brother's murdered.

Once upon a Time in the West 1968   ★ ★ ★ ★

Sergio Leone's testament to the wild west, with *Henry Fonda* cast (unusually) as cold-blooded killer.

One-Eyed Jacks 1961   ★ ★ ★

Outlaw, *Marlon Brando*, seeks revenge on double-crossing partner, *Karl Malden*. Moody atmosphere prevails.

Outlaw, The 1943   ★ ★

Once notoriously sexy, now tame, western. *Jane Russell* almost tumbling out of her bra during tumble with Billy the Kid.

Outlaw Josey Wales, The 1976   ★ ★ ★ ★

Last great western ever made. *Clint Eastwood* plays family man turned vigilante when wife and kids are murdered by union soldiers.

Pale Rider 1985   ★ ★ ★

Enigmatic, slightly pretentious western. *Clint Eastwood* as avenging angel cleaning up corrupt town.

WES

Quigley Down Under 1990

Tom Selleck arrives in turn-of-century Australia as trouble shooter for evil ranch owner, *Alan Rickman*. A western down under.

Red River 1948

Epic movie by Howard Hawkes. A cattle drive sparks conflict between leader, *John Wayne*, and rebel, *Montgomery Clift*.

Rio Bravo 1959

Howard Hawk's affectionate tribute in which ill-assorted quartet of lawmen, hired guns and drunks fight off bad guys.

Rio Grande 1950

Last of John Ford's splendid cavalry trilogy. *John Wayne* licks new Cavalry recruits - one of them his son - into shape in post-Civil War era.

Searchers, The 1956

The finest of all Westerns. Racist *John Wayne* seeks his niece, *Natalie Wood*, kidnapped by marauding Indians, in order to kill her. *Jeffrey Hunter* wants to save her.

Shane 1953

One of the classic westerns. *Alan Ladd's* arrival disturbs the lives of the homesteaders he's come to protect. *Jack Palance* marvellous as the chief heavy.

She Wore a Yellow Ribbon 1949

Lavish, satisfying homage from the master, John Ford. Aging cavalry officer, *John Wayne*, reluctant to retire while the Apaches are on the war-path.

Shootist, The 1976

Touching performance by *John Wayne* as dying gunfighter looking for a place to lay his holster. *James Stewart* and *Lauren Bacall* also feature. Deeply nostalgic.

Silverado 1985 ★ ★

Low-key homage to the old west with *Kevin Kline*, *Kevin Costner* and *John Cleese*.

Stagecoach 1939 ★ ★ ★ ★ ★

The ultimate western from John Ford with *John Wayne* as the Ringo Kid, *Claire Trevor*, the-tart-with-a-heart, aboard a stage-coach threatened by Red Indians.

Support Your Local Sheriff! 1969 ★ ★ ★

Charming parody pits reluctant sheriff, *James Garner*, against lawless mining town, as he drifts through on his way to Australia.

They Died with Their Boots On 1941 ★ ★ ★

Hollywood's lavish, whitewashed version of the Little Bighorn battle with *Errol Flynn* as Colonel Custer, *Olivia de Haviland* his worried wife.

True Grit 1969

John Wayne's only Oscar-winning performance as crusty old marshal helping young girl get revenge for father's death.

Wild Bunch, The 1969 ★ ★ ★ ★

Violent, rivetting Sam Peckinpah western set in 1914, when the few remaining outlaws find the rules have changed.

Winchester '73 1950

Fine, intelligent example of the genre. *James Stewart* tracks his stolen gun across the prairies.

Young Guns 1988

Brat Pack western explores the romantic myth surrounding Billy the Kid. *Keifer Sutherland*, *Charlie Sheen* and *Emilio Estevez* (as Billy) are the young outlaws.

Young Guns II 1990 ★ ★

Pretty fair sequel to the above. *Christian Slater* joins cast, Charlie Sheen leaves it. Rest of team remains the same.

WES

A

B

C

D

CHOSEN YOUR VIDEO...

...NOW PICK UP YOUR PIZZA

Pizza Hut bake every pizza fresh to order using only the choicest ingredients. Try an Hawaiian, Cheese Feast, Meat Feast or the ultimate Super Supreme. There is also Garlic Bread and Pepsi for a perfect ending.

Phone Pizza Hut with your order and if you live in a delivery area they will deliver within 30 minutes or you can collect your pizza in 20 minutes. If the delivery is late Pizza Hut will give you £1 off your order.

Check the store listing for your nearest Pizza Hut or look in your local Yellow Pages.

MARGHERITA Classic Mozzarella cheese and tomato

HAWAIIAN Ham and pineapple

VEGETARIAN Mushrooms, green peppers and onions

SEAFARER Tuna, prawns and tomato

SPICY HOT ONE Green chilli, beef topping, onion and tomato

PEPPERONI FEAST Double decker pepperoni layered with a special blend of 3 cheeses - Mozzarella, Cheddar and Monterey Jack

MEAT FEAST 4 meaty toppings, spicy pork, ham, pepperoni and beef topping covered with 3 cheeses - Mozzarella, Cheddar and Monterey Jack

COUNTRY FEAST A feast of mushrooms, green peppers, onion, tomato and sweetcorn topped with a special blend of 3 cheeses - Mozzarella, Cheddar and Monterey Jack

CHEESE FEAST A feast of a special blend of 3 cheeses - Mozzarella, Cheddar and Monterey Jack plus ANY 2 of your favourite toppings

SUPREME Pepperoni, mushroom, green pepper, onion and beef topping

SUPER SUPREME Spicy pork, pepperoni, mushroom, ham, green pepper, onion, black olives and beef topping

CREATE YOUR OWN Pan Pizza with special tomato sauce and Mozzarella cheese

Each additional topping of your choice

Spicy Pork Onion Mushroom Green Chilli Green Peppers Tuna Extra Cheese Ham Anchovy Beef Topping Prawns Black Olives Tomato Pepperoni Pineapple Sweetcorn

YOU CAN ALSO ORDER

GARLIC BREAD 4-pieces

GARLIC BREAD SUPREME Topped with melted Mozzarella 4-pieces

PEPSI or **DIET PEPSI** 1.5 litre bottle

Limited delivery area. Please note drivers only carry £10 in change.
All items subject to availability

149

● = Delivery Service Available

CENTRAL LONDON

ARGYLL STREET 12 Argyll Street 071 434 1542
● BAKER STREET 66 Baker Street 071 935 6125
CAMBRIDGE CIRCUS Cambridge Circus 071 379 4655
DUKE STREET 67 Duke Street 071 629 0030
EARL'S COURT 149 Earl's Court Road 071 370 3066
● FULHAM 654b Fulham Road 071 371 5030
HAYMARKET 53 Haymarket 071 839 5041
● KING'S ROAD 56 King's Road 071 581 5517
LEICESTER SQUARE 19 Leicester Square 071 930 9114
MARBLE ARCH 523 Oxford Street 071 493 6427
OXFORD STREET 29 Oxford Street 071 434 3934
OXFORD STREET 79 Oxford Street 071 734 4534
● PIMLICO 113 Lupus Street 071 976 5722
QUEENSWAY 103 Queensway 071 221 6443
● STRAND 56 The Strand 071 925 0050
SWISS COTTAGE 149 Finchley Road 071 722 8182
VICTORIA 74 Victoria Street 071 821 5533

GREATER LONDON

● ACTON 78 High Street 081 752 0303
● ASHFORD 349 Staines Road West 0784 240506
● BARKING 89 Longbridge Road 081 594 8505
● BOREHAMWOOD 26 Shenley Road 081 905 1888
● BRIXTON 467 Brixton Road 071 978 8248
● CATFORD 10 The Broadway 081 690 9737
● CHISWICK 404 Chiswick High Road 081 747 3688
● CLAPHAM 75 Abbeville Road 081 675 8640
● CLAPHAM JUNCTION St John's Hill 071 924 1855
● CROUCH END 34 Topsfield Prd., Tottenham La. 081 348 4455
● DENMARK HILL 57 Denmark Hill 071 277 0674
● DOWNHAM 14 Bromley Hill 081 313 1441
● EALING 39 New Broadway 081 567 1114
EALING 64 The Mall 081 567 9798
● EALING WEST 66 Broadway 081 579 5845
● EARLSFIELD 174 Garrett Lane 081 877 0877
● EAST FINCHLEY 70 High Road 081 442 1122
● EAST HAM 11 High Street North 081 471 5292
● EAST SHEEN 160 Upper Richmond Road West 081 876 1234
● ELTHAM 19 High Street 081 850 9977
● FINCHLEY 128 Ballards Lane 081 349 4448
● FOREST GATE 60 Woodgrange Road 081 519 5100
● GOLDERS GREEN 18 North End Road 081 201 9800
● GREENFORD 197 Greenford Road 081 575 5888
● HAMMERSMITH 100 King Street 081 748 2006
HAMPSTEAD 60 High Street 071 431 0414
● HARRINGEY 42 Grand Parade, Green Lanes 081 802 9626
● HARROW WEALD 254 High Road 081 424 8800
● HENDON 112 Brent Street 081 202 1858
HOLLOWAY 12 Seven Sisters Road 071 609 8481
● HOUNSLOW 11 High Street 081 570 5657

● HOUNSLOW WEST 292 Bath Road 081 569 4004
● ISLINGTON 169 Upper Street 071 354 5055
ISLINGTON 77 Upper Street 071 359 0987
● KENTISH TOWN 120 Fortess Road 071 284 4080
● KEW 94 Kew Road 081 332 0666
● KILBURN 238 Kilburn High Road 071 328 9809
● KINGSBURY 497 Kingsbury Road 081 206 2233
● LEE GREEN 115 Burnt Ash Road 081 297 1000
LEWISHAM 54 High Street 081 318 9115
● MILL HILL 111 Mill Hill Broadway 081 906 1616
● NORBURY 1374 London Road 081 765 0202
● PALMERS GREEN 409 Green Lanes 081 882 6662
● PENGE 126/128 High Street 081 778 8686
● PUTNEY 31 High Street 081 785 2351
● RAYNERS LANE 420 Alexandra Avenue 081 868 1244
● RUISLIP MANOR 30 Victoria Road 0895 621188
SHEPHERD'S BUSH 15/19 Goldhawk Road 081 746 1300
● SOUTHGATE 2 Hampden Square 081 361 3193
STAMFORD HILL 198 Stamford Hill 081 809 3838
STRATFORD 52/54 The Broadway 081 519 9966
STREATHAM 112 Streatham Hill 081 671 7311
● SUDBURY 151 Greenford Road 081 864 8012
● TOOTING 86 Mitcham Road 081 682 2323
TOOTING 16 Tooting High Street 081 767 4816
● UPPER NORWOOD Westow Street 081 771 8343
● WALTHAMSTOW 106 High Street 081 521 1211
● WALTHAMSTOW 253/255 High Street 081 503 6666
WALWORTH 318 Walworth Road 071 703 9813
● WEST NORWOOD 24 Knights Hill 081 766 6464
● WEST WICKHAM 38 Glebe Way 081 777 5544
WHITECHAPEL 245 Whitechapel Road 071 247 9958
● WHITTON 25 High Street 081 893 3003
● WILLESDEN 7 Walm Lane 081 451 2244
● WIMBLEDON 48 The Broadway 081 543 7077
● WOOD GREEN 183 High Road 081 888 2282
● WOODFORD GREEN 3 Rex Prd., Snakes La. 081 504 9595
● WOOLWICH 83 Powis Street 081 854 4460
● YIEWSLEY 134 High Street 0895 421321

BERKS

BRACKNELL 1 Princess Square 0344 411844
● MAIDENHEAD 5 The Colonnade 0628 36245
● NEWBURY 41 North Brook Street 0635 551234
READING 6 Oxford Road 0734 586086
● READING Unit 5 Oxford Road 0734 451100
SLOUGH 59 Queensmere Centre 0753 530311
WINDSOR 19 Thames Street 0753 840247

EAST ANGLIA

● BURY ST EDMUNDS 2 Cornhill 0284 701201
● CAMBRIDGE 19 Regent Street 0223 323737
CAMBRIDGE 66 St Andrews Street 0223 323616
● COLCHESTER 48 High Street 0206 574478
● GT. YARMOUTH 3 Regent Road 0493 330933
● IPSWICH 45 Upper Brook Street 0473 216922

NORWICH 27 Orford Place 0603 760121
● PETERBOROUGH Carr Road Boongate 0733 892929

ESSEX
● BASILDON 5 East Square 0268 531475
● BRENTWOOD 16 High Street 0277 217511
● CHELMSFORD Chelmer Village Retail Park 0245 496490
● DAGENHAM 339 Valence Avenue 081 598 1414
  HARLOW 27 Eastgate 0279 641464
● HARLOW Unit 13 Harlow Retail Park 0279 437711
● HORNCHURCH 46 High Street 04024 74073
● ILFORD 198 High Road 081 553 2782
● ILFORD 86/88 Cranbrook Road 081 553 3388
  LOUGHTON 2 Centric Parade 200 High Street 081 502 5300
● RAINHAM 47 Upminster Road South 0708 630220
● ROMFORD 101 South Street 0708 742256
● SOUTHEND 14 South Church Road 0702 618206
● S. WOODFORD 25 Electric Prd., George La. 081 532 9077
● WEST THURROCK Lakeside Retail Park 0708 869155

HANTS / SUSSEX / DORSET
● ALDERSHOT 107 High Street 0252 25796
  BOURNEMOUTH 82 Old Christchurch Road 0202 298537
● BRIGHTON 81 Western Road 0273 27991
● BRIGHTON 58 London Road 0273 608217
● CRAWLEY 38 High Street 0293 553687
● EASTLEIGH 33 Leigh Road 0703 629255
● FARNBOROUGH 98 Queensmead 0252 522505
● PORTSMOUTH 97 Commercial Road 0705 829638
  SOUTHAMPTON 21 Hanover Buildings 0703 224909
● SOUTHAMPTON 190 Portswood Road 0703 582627
  SOUTHSEA 77 Palmerston Road 0705 862323
● WINCHESTER 7 High Street 0962 841155
● WORTHING 8 South Street 0903 230494

HERTS / BEDS / BUCKS
● BARNET 98/100 High Street 081 441 5553
● BARNET 30 East Barnet Road 081 449 1041
● BEDFORD 68 High Street 0234 271575
  BEDFORD Aspects Leisure Park, Newnham Ave 0234 363314
● BISHOP'S STORTFORD 1 Potter Street 0279 755744
● CHESHUNT 15 Newham Parade, College Road 0992 22229
● DUNSTABLE 48 High Street North 0582 471094
● HATFIELD 1 Town Centre 07072 72551
  HIGH WYCOMBE 15 White Hart Street 0494 450757
● HODDESDON 29 High Street 0992 451040
● LETCHWORTH 21b Eastcheap 0462 482224
● LUTON 12 Park Square 0582 456958
  MILTON KEYNES Milton Keynes Shopping Ctr. 0908 233222
● ST ALBANS 81 St Peter's Street 0727 44442
● STEVENAGE Roaring Meg Retail Park 0438 740707
● WALTHAM CROSS 76 High Street 0992 700239
● WATFORD 474 St Albans Road 0923 817611
● WATFORD The Parade, The High Street 0923 225362
● WELWYN GARDEN CITY I Howardsgate 0707 332264

KENT
● ASHFORD 1 High Street 0233 640520
● BECKENHAM 145 High Street 081 650 5500
● BEXLEYHEATH 113 The Broadway 081 298 0088
  BROMLEY 21 High Street 081 290 0377
  CANTERBURY 39 High Street 0227 451049
  DARTFORD 12 Hythe Street 0322 289353
● FOLKSTONE 4 Guildhall Street, Market Square 0303 851172
  MAIDSTONE 63 High Street 0622 686354
  MARGATE 38 High Street 0843 296419
● ORPINGTON 243 High Street 0689 872921
● SIDCUP 104 High Street 081 308 1880
● ST MARY'S CRAY 28/28a Marion Crescent 0689 874850
● TUNBRIDGE WELLS 45 Mount Pleasant Road 0892 515685

MIDDLESEX
  EDGWARE 151 Station Road 081 952 8928
● ENFIELD 37 The Town 081 367 2259
● HARROW 370 Station Road 081 861 1515
● HAYES 832 Uxbridge Road 081 561 3000
  RUISLIP 85 High Street 0895 621621
● SOUTHALL Unit B 62 The Broadway 081 893 5252
● TWICKENHAM 33/35 London Road 081 744 1133
  UXBRIDGE 148 High Street 0895 272526
● WEMBLEY 452 High Road 081 900 2288

OXON / NORTHANTS
● BANBURY 33 High Street 0295 270044
● NORTHAMPTON 71 Abingdon Street 0604 20826
● NORTHAMPTON St James's Retail Park 0604 603666
  OXFORD 61 George Street 0865 790089

SOUTH WEST
  BATH 1 Westgate Buildings 0225 448586
● BRISTOL 2 Penn Street, Broadmead 0272 272916
  BRISTOL 23 St Augustine's Parade 0272 252755
  CHELTENHAM 5 Promenade 0242 577455
  GLOUCESTER Unit 8, Peel Centre, Bristol Rd 0452 330033
● SALISBURY 40 Blue Boar Row 0722 411099
● SWINDON Shaw Ridge Leisure Park 0793 876212
  TORQUAY 79 Fleet Walk, Fleet Road 0803 200440

SURREY
● CARSHALTON 14 Green Wrythe Lane 081 669 9539
● CATERHAM 6 The Square 0883 347334
● CHESSINGTON 377 Hook Road 081 974 1522
● COULSDON 84 Brighton Road 081 763 1234
  CROYDON 38 George Street 081 681 5953
● CROYDON 30 London Road 081 688 7771
  CROYDON 61 North End 081 680 1086
● EPSOM 9 High Street 03727 27272
  GUILDFORD 12 North Street 0483 300501
● MORDEN 9 Morden Court Parade 081 687 1313
● NEW MALDEN 160 High Street 081 336 1333
  RICHMOND 30 Hill Street 081 940 3328

SUTTON 55 High Street 081 661 6160
- TOLWORTH 20 Broadway 081 390 5556
- WALTON-ON-THAMES 35 The Centre 0932 243522
- WOKING 19 Chertsey Road 0483 755845

WALES
CARDIFF 28 High Street 0222 371557
NEWPORT 9 Bridge Street 0633 216335
SWANSEA 62 The Kingsway 0792 648585

MIDLANDS
BIRMINGHAM 41 New Street 021 631 4855
BIRMINGHAM 66 New Street 021 643 8778
BIRMINGHAM 16 Colmore Row 021 236 7808
BIRMINGHAM Arcadian Centre 021 622 7479
- BRADFORD 2 Duckworth Grove 0274 482313
- BRADFORD 463 Otley Road 0274 642020
- BROMSGROVE 14 High Street 0527 579379
- BURTON-UPON-TRENT 167 High Street 0283 511770
- CHESTERFIELD 16 Packers Row 0246 221662
COVENTRY 2 Ironmonger Row 0203 226116
- DERBY 17 Cornmarket 0332 371719
- DRONFIELD 49 Chesterfield Road 0246 290318
- DUDLEY Merry Hill Centre 0384 263844
- KEIGHLEY Unit 2, 25/29 Cavendish Street 0535 611602
- LEAMINGTON SPA 140 The Parade 0926 831225
- LEICESTER 6 The Haymarket 0533 512422
- NOTTINGHAM 609 Mansfield Road 0602 691155
- NOTTINGHAM 26 Oakdale Road 0602 401055
NOTTINGHAM 7 The Poultry 0602 501446
NOTTINGHAM 30 Market Street 0602 410123
- NUNEATON 6 Abbey Street 0203 641810
- SHIRLEY UCI Cinema Complex, Stratford Road 021 733 3457
- STAPLEFORD 148 Derby Road 0602 490011
STOKE-ON-TRENT Festival Park 0782 289900
STRATFORD-UPON-AVON 23 High Street 0789 204182
- TELFORD Unit 12, Telford Bridge Retail Park 0952 293470
- WEST BRIDGFORD Unit 1, Gordon Road 0602 455566
WEST BROMWICH The Farley Centre 021 500 5232
WOLVERHAMPTON 10 Victoria Street 0902 710066

NORTH EAST
- COLLIER ROW 3 Chase Cross Road 0708 761376
- DARLINGTON 4 Horsemarket 0325 357711
- DONCASTER 19 High Street 0302 322223
GATESHEAD Metro Centre 091 493 2161
HULL 58 Jameson Street 0482 218616
- MIDDLESBROUGH 99 Linthorp Road 0642 231656
NEWCASTLE-UPON-TYNE 66 Grainger Street 091 232 0790
- SUNDERLAND Waterloo Way 091 510 0499

NORTH WEST
- ALTRINCHAM 7 Cross Street 061 926 8059
- BLACKBURN 59 King William Street 0254 680345
- BLACKPOOL 7 Church Street 0253 28883
BLACKPOOL Unit 3, 4 Ocean Blvd, S. Shore 0253 407307
- BURNLEY 34/36 St James Street 0282 416509
- BURY 30 Haymarket Street 061 764 7375
- CARLISLE Lowther Street 0228 590066
- CHESTER 83 Foregate Street 0244 346991
- DIDSBURY 766 Wilmslow Road 061 434 9920
LIVERPOOL Unit 8b, Blacklees, Gt Charlotte St. 051 708 0049
- MANCHESTER 27 St Mary's Gate 061 834 8684
MANCHESTER 6 Fountain Street 061 834 5877
MANCHESTER 67 Oxford Street 061 236 0779
- MANCHESTER White City Retail Pk, Chester Rd. 061 876 0770
PRESTON 30 Cheapside 0772 201747
- ROCHDALE 20/22 Yorkshire Street 0706 46444
SOUTHPORT 347 Lord Street 0704 548434
- STOCKPORT 10 Grand Central 061 476 6606
- WARRINGTON Alban Retail Park, Winwick Road 0925 574220

SCOTLAND
- ABERDEEN 7 Union Bridge 0224 573363
DUNDEE 2/4 Nethergate 0382 200220
EDINBURGH 34 Hanover Street 031 226 3652
EDINBURGH 46 North Bridge 031 226 3038
EDINBURGH 113/117 Lothian Road 031 228 2920
FALKIRK 37 High Street 0324 34138
GLASGOW 203 Argyle Street 041 221 0144
GLASGOW 85 West George Street 041 226 3633

YORKSHIRE
- BINGLEY 125 Main Street 0274 562555
BIRSTALL Centre 27 Business Park 0924 420460
BRADFORD 7 Cheapside 0274 736284
GRIMSBY 68 Victoria Street 0472 242999
HALIFAX 36 Southgate 0422 345015
- HARROGATE 19 Parliament Street 0423 524396
HUDDERSFIELD 6-8 John William Street 0484 427030
LEEDS 33 Briggate 0532 448701
- LEEDS 37 Harrogate Road 0532 629955
- LEEDS 174 Selby Road 0532 600300
SCARBOROUGH 4 Huntriss Row 0723 360706
SHEFFIELD 12 Wellington Street 0742 752012
- SHEFFIELD 1/3 Berkley Precinct, Ecclesall Rd. 0742 680697
- SHEFFIELD 381 Abbeydale Road 0742 554903
- SHEFFIELD Unit 1, Lound Court, Chapeltown 0742 454546
WAKEFIELD 9 Bread Street 0924 367169
YORK 14 Clifford Street 0904 646361
YORK 10 Pavement 0904 636966

● = Delivery Service Available

HALF PRICE PIZZA

Buy any medium or large speciality
pizza and get another up to the same
value for 1/2 price

1 Offer valid until the 31st December 1992
2 Only one voucher per order.
3 Not to be used in conjunction with any other offer.
4 Both Pizzas to be ordered at the same time.

GARLIC BREAD SPECIAL

FREE

portion of Garlic Bread when your
purchase any large Pizza.

1 Offer valid until the 31st December 1992
2 Only one voucher per order.
3 Not to be used in conjunction with any other offer.